Adult Coloring Book

Henna Paisley Designs #3

ISBN-13: 978-1532708459

ISBN-10: 1532708459

All enquiries, contact

Hobby Habitat Coloring

contact@hobbyhabitat.com

Get a FREE Coloring Book

Coloring book fan?

Get a free coloring book from the website bellow:

www.hobbyhabitat.com/freecoloringbook

Hello and thank you for buying our third Henna Paisley Adult Coloring Book!

Why three books? Because we hope you will agree when we say that Henna Paisley patterns are some of the most beautiful but also challenging design one can use for coloring.

This book as well as our previous adult coloring books has a range of designs, from simple ones, excellent for beginner colorists up to some very intricate designs perfect for experienced coloring enthusiasts.

We hope that you will enjoy coloring these wonderful stress relieving patterns as much as we enjoyed putting them together for you.

Once again thank you for buying our book, and enjoy coloring with Hobby Habitat's adult coloring books.

Thank you!

Hobby Habitat Coloring Books

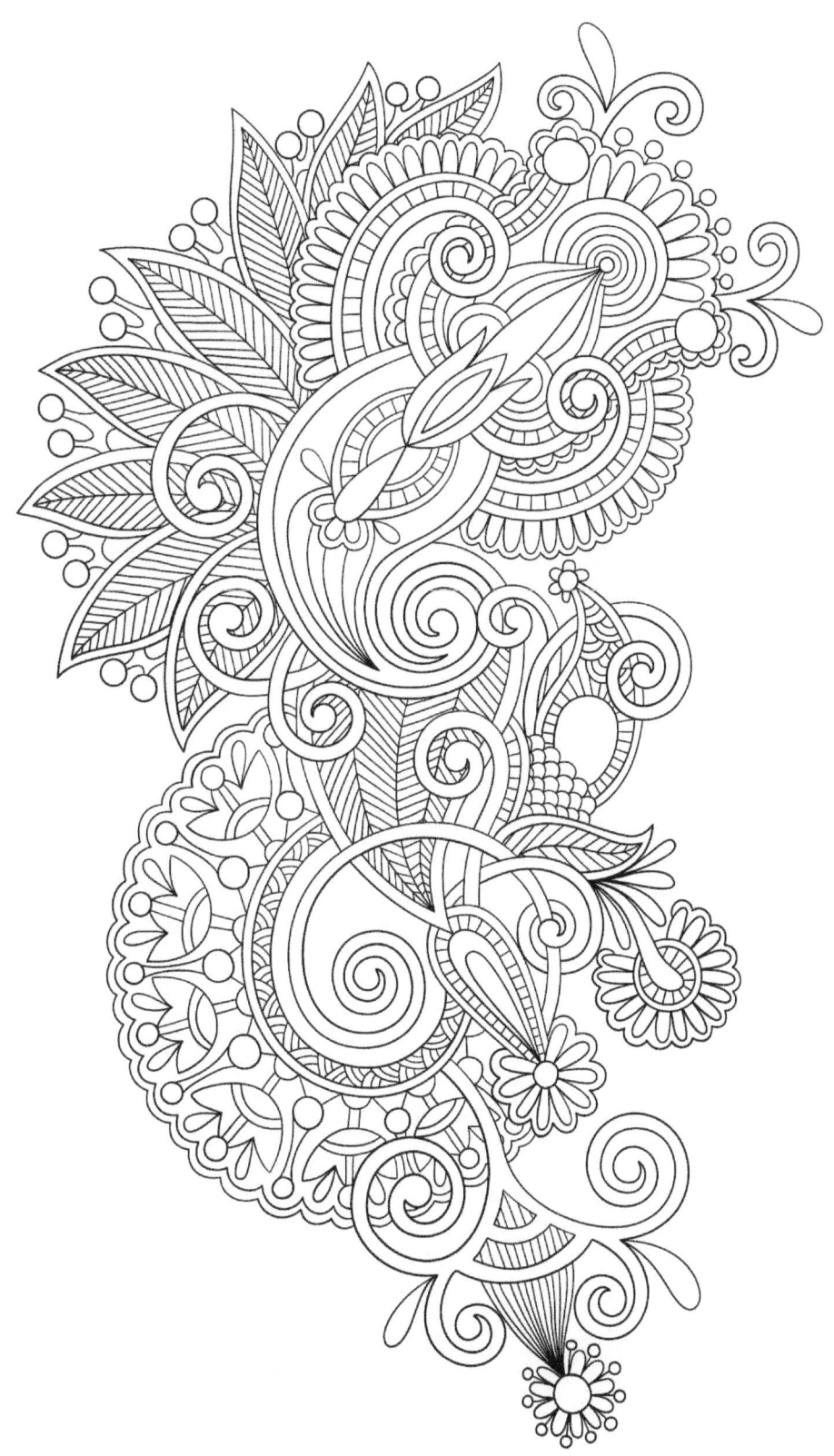

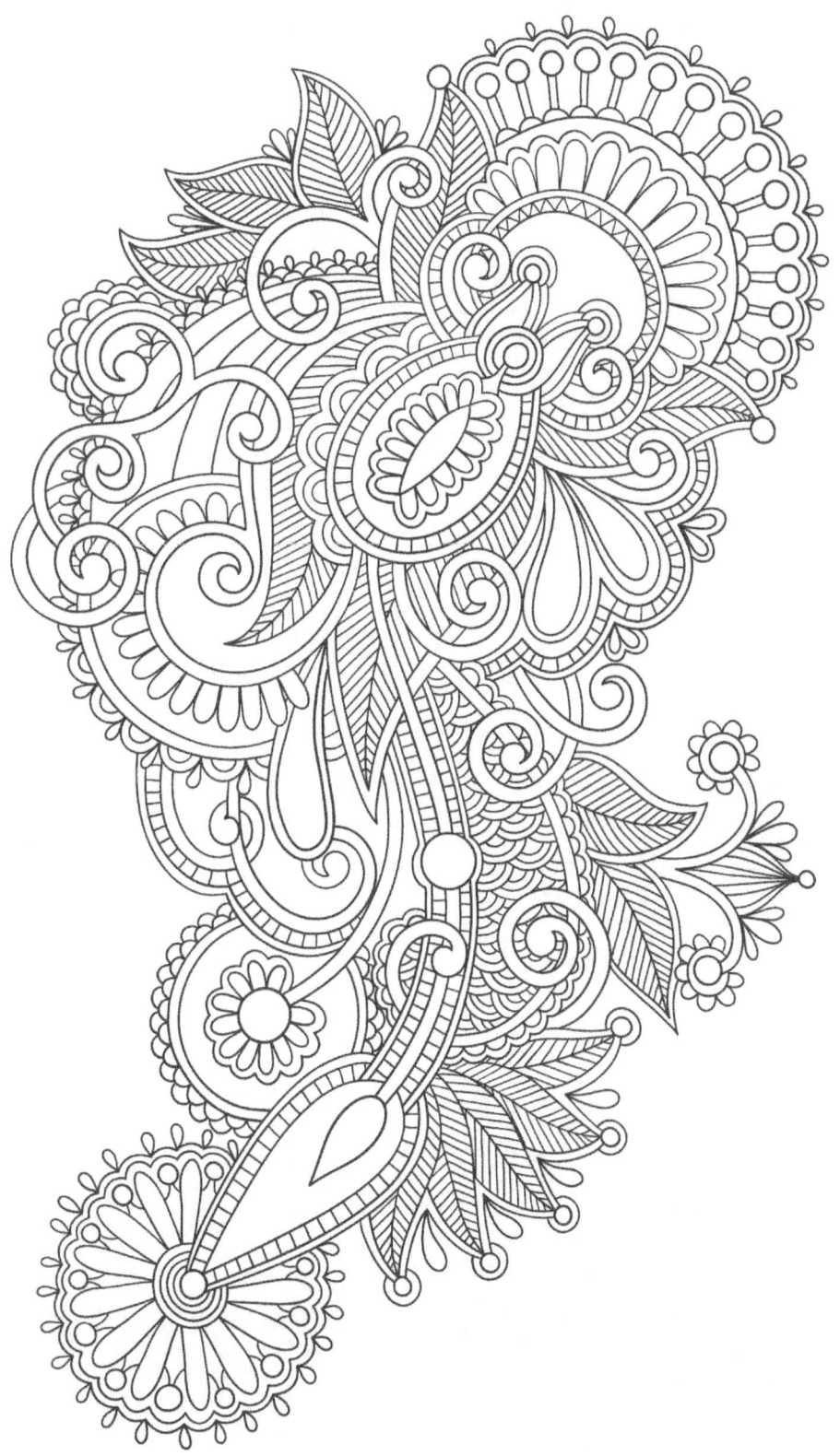

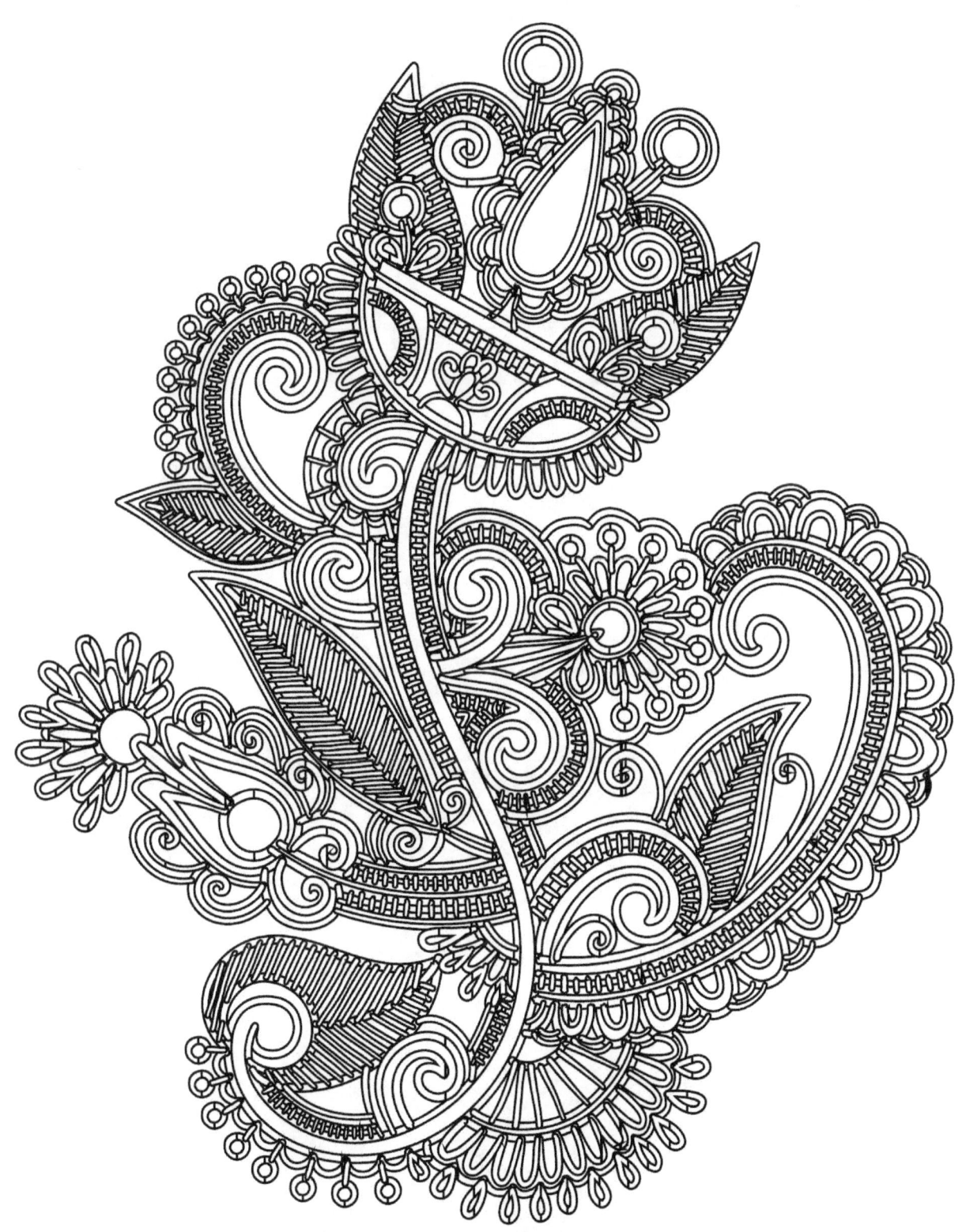

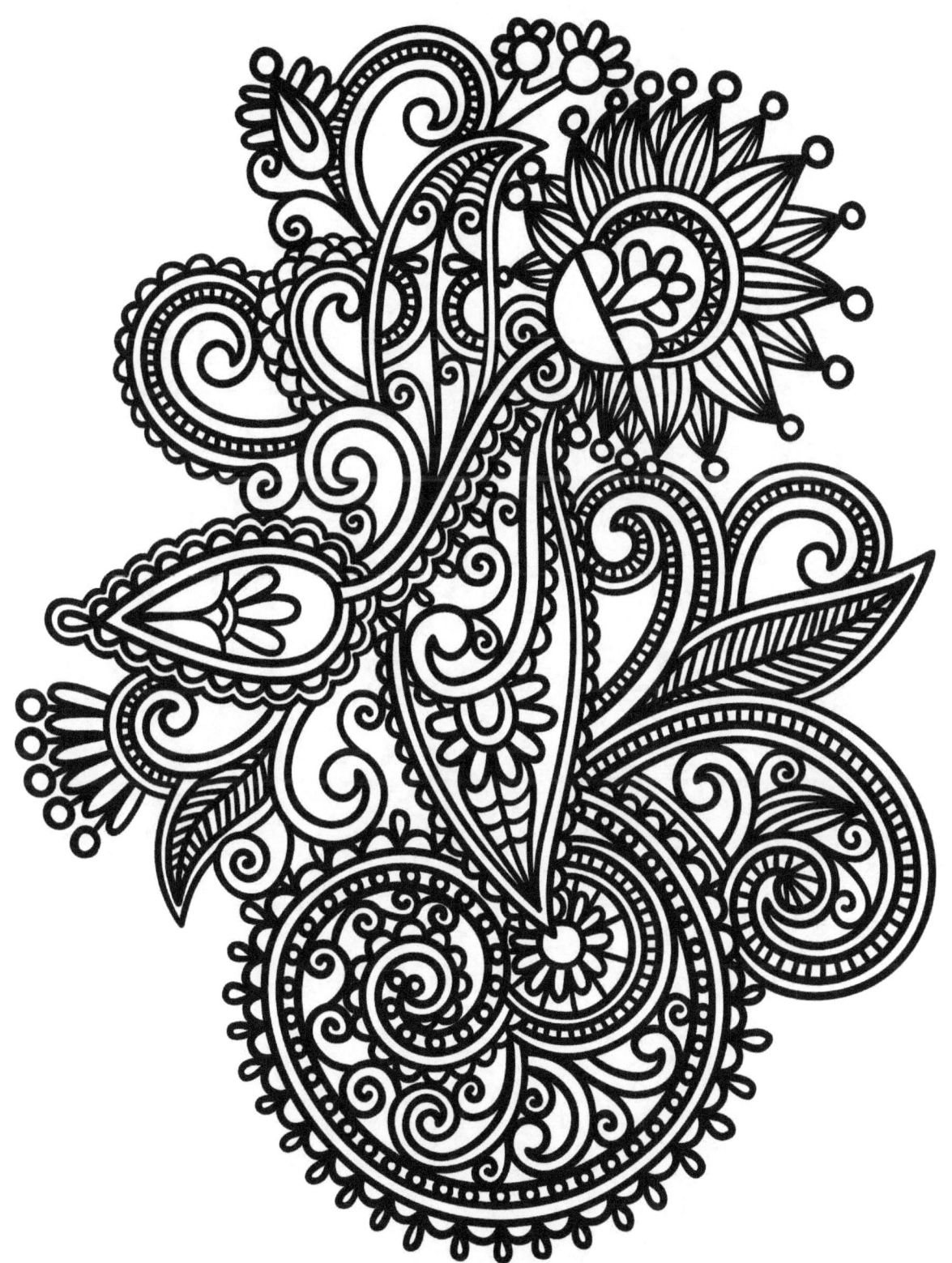

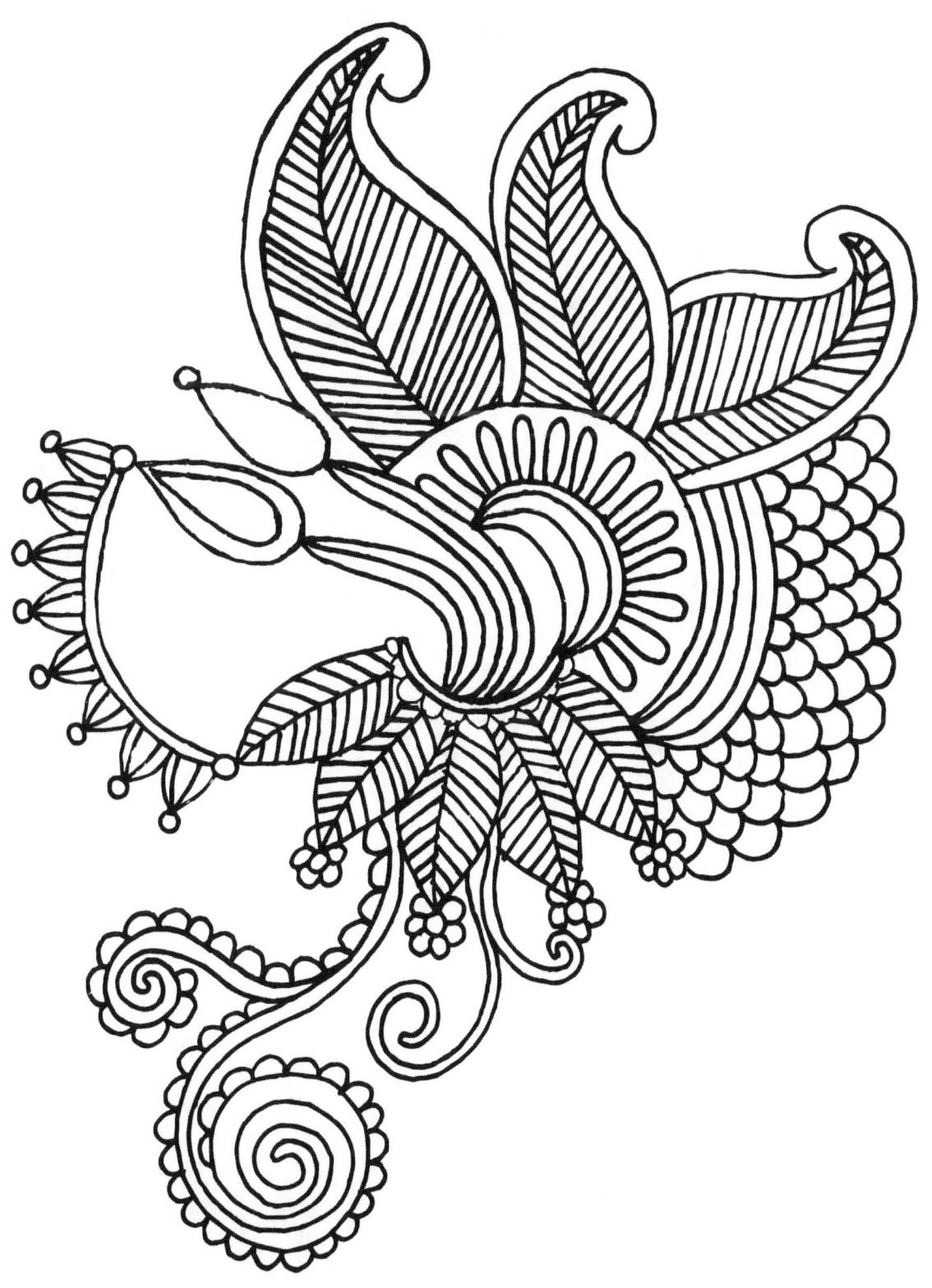

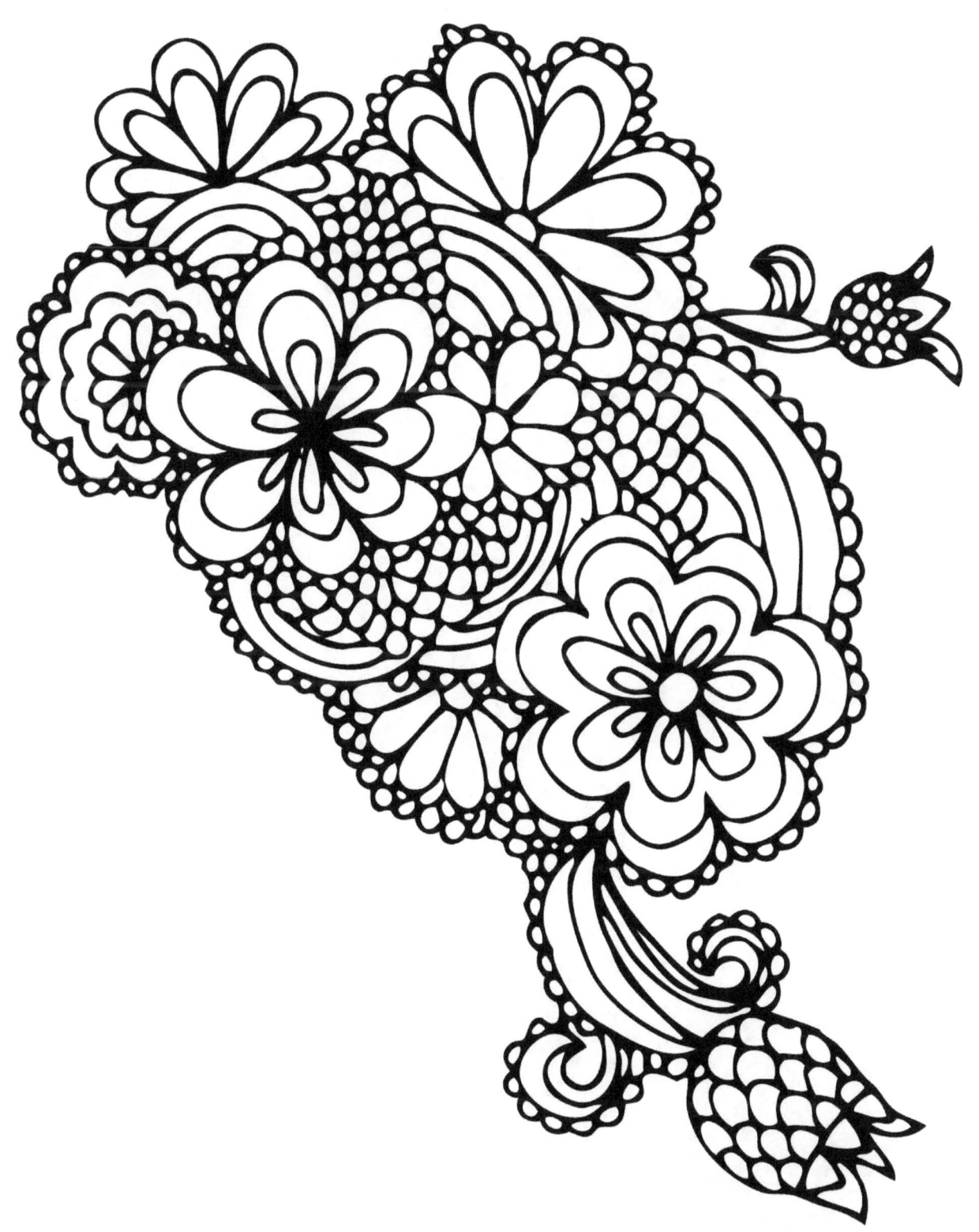

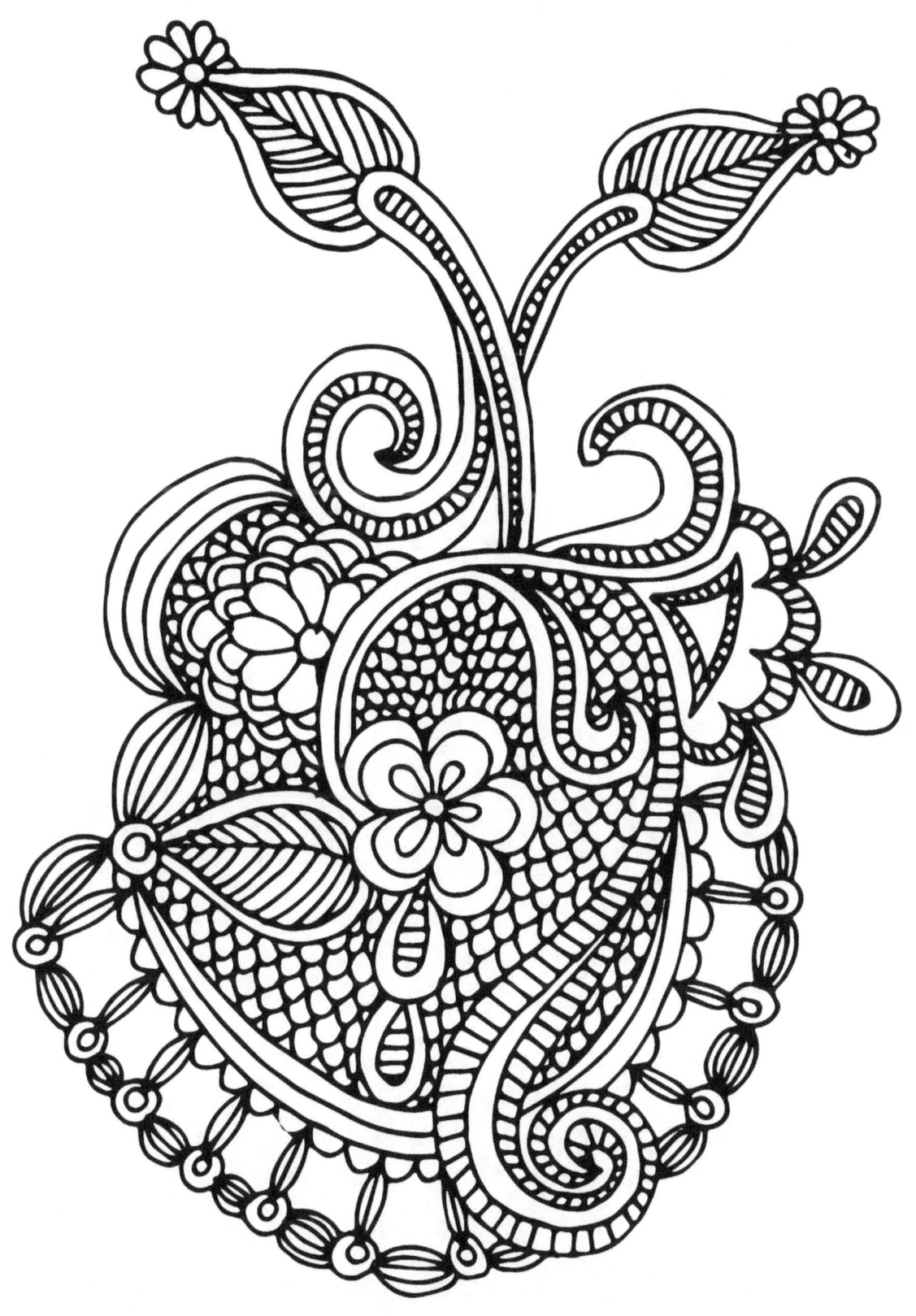

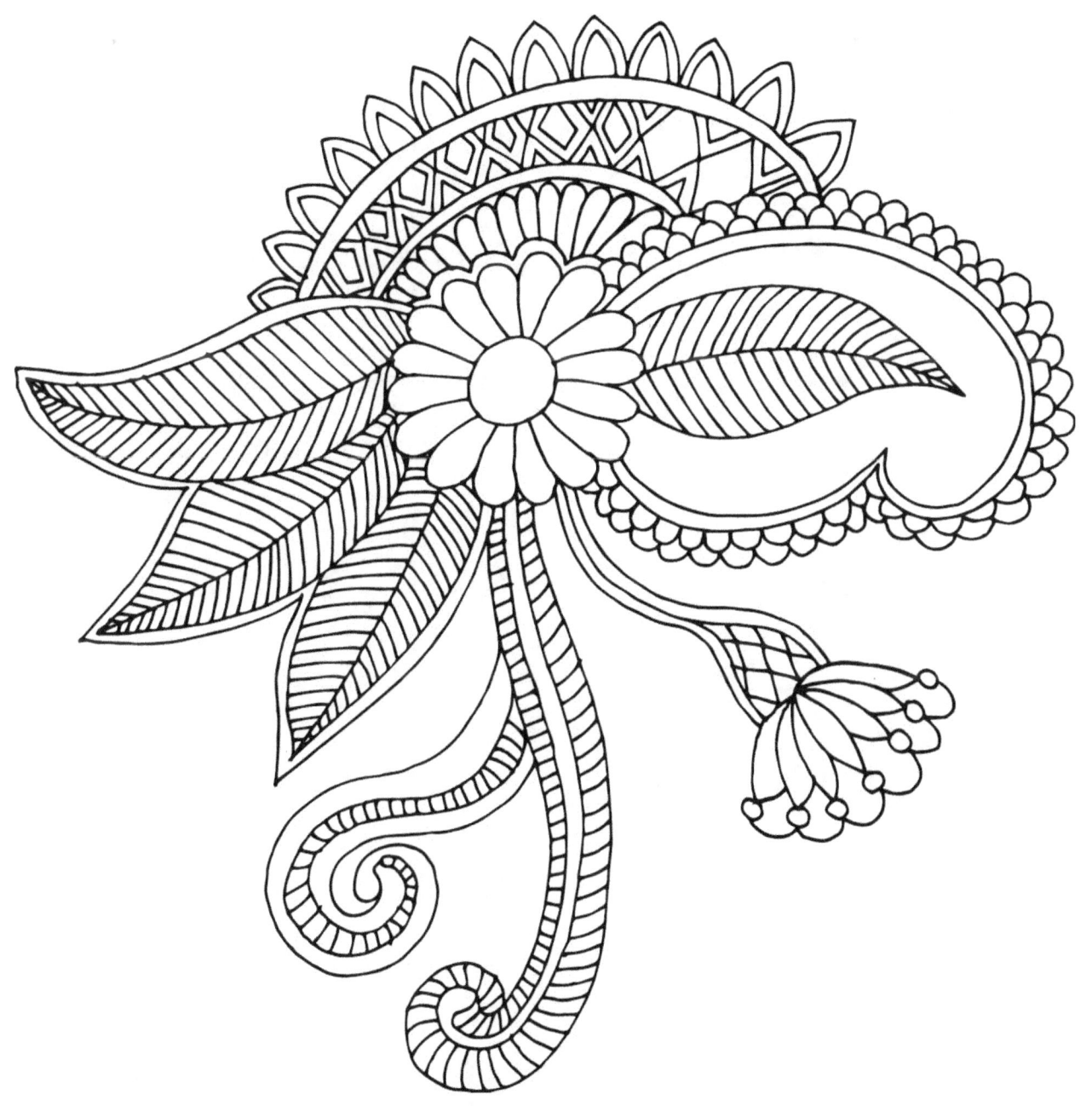

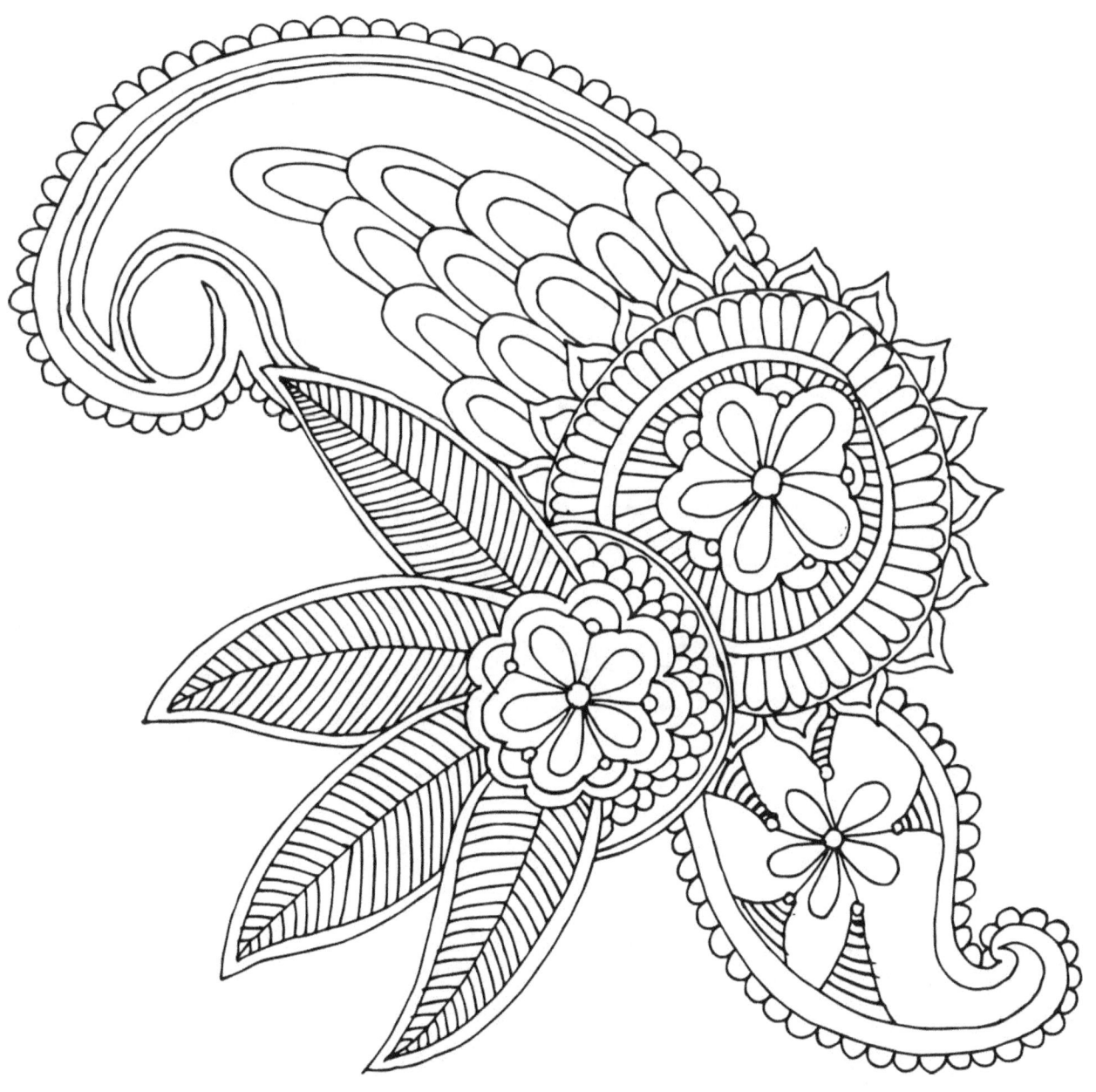

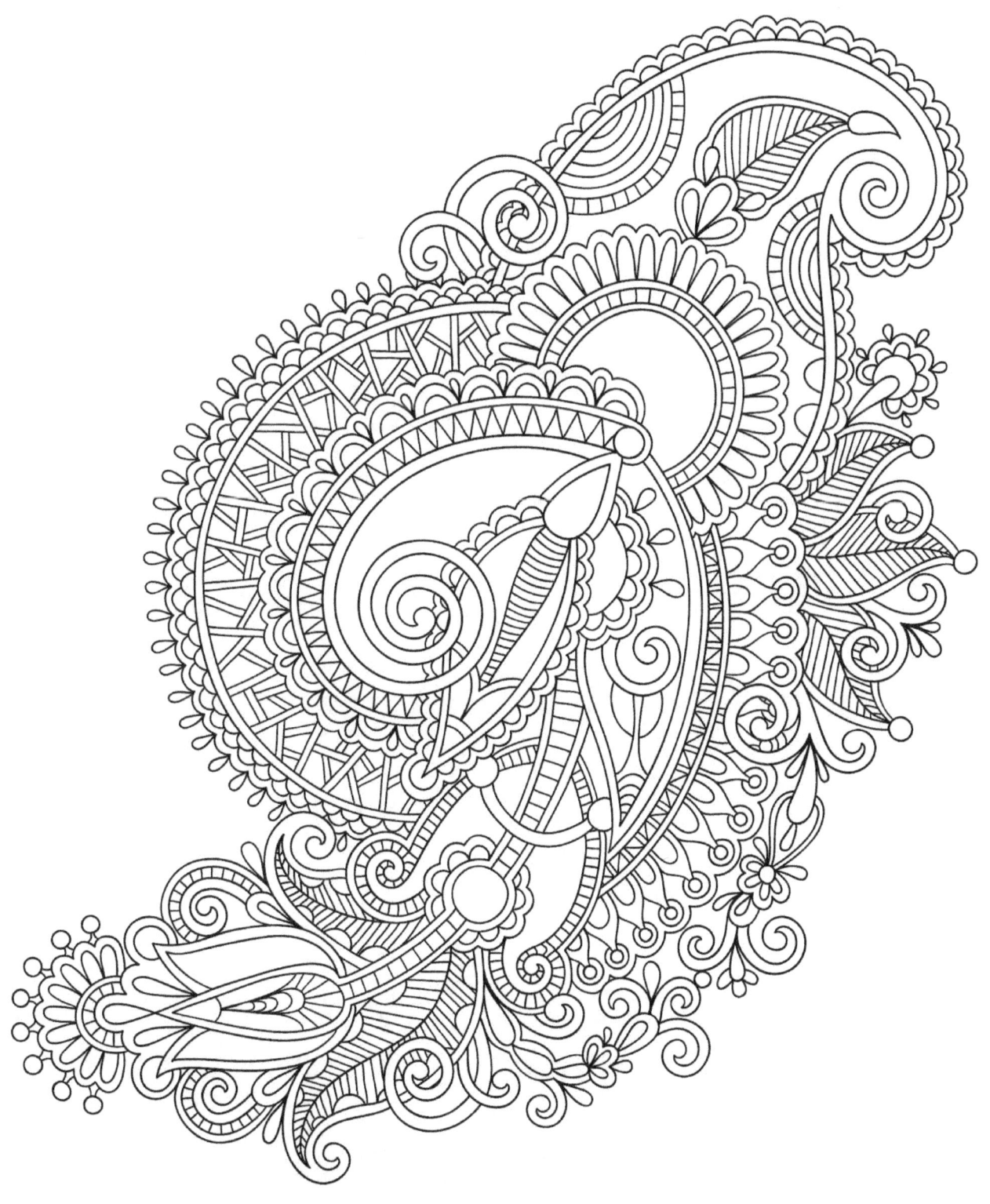

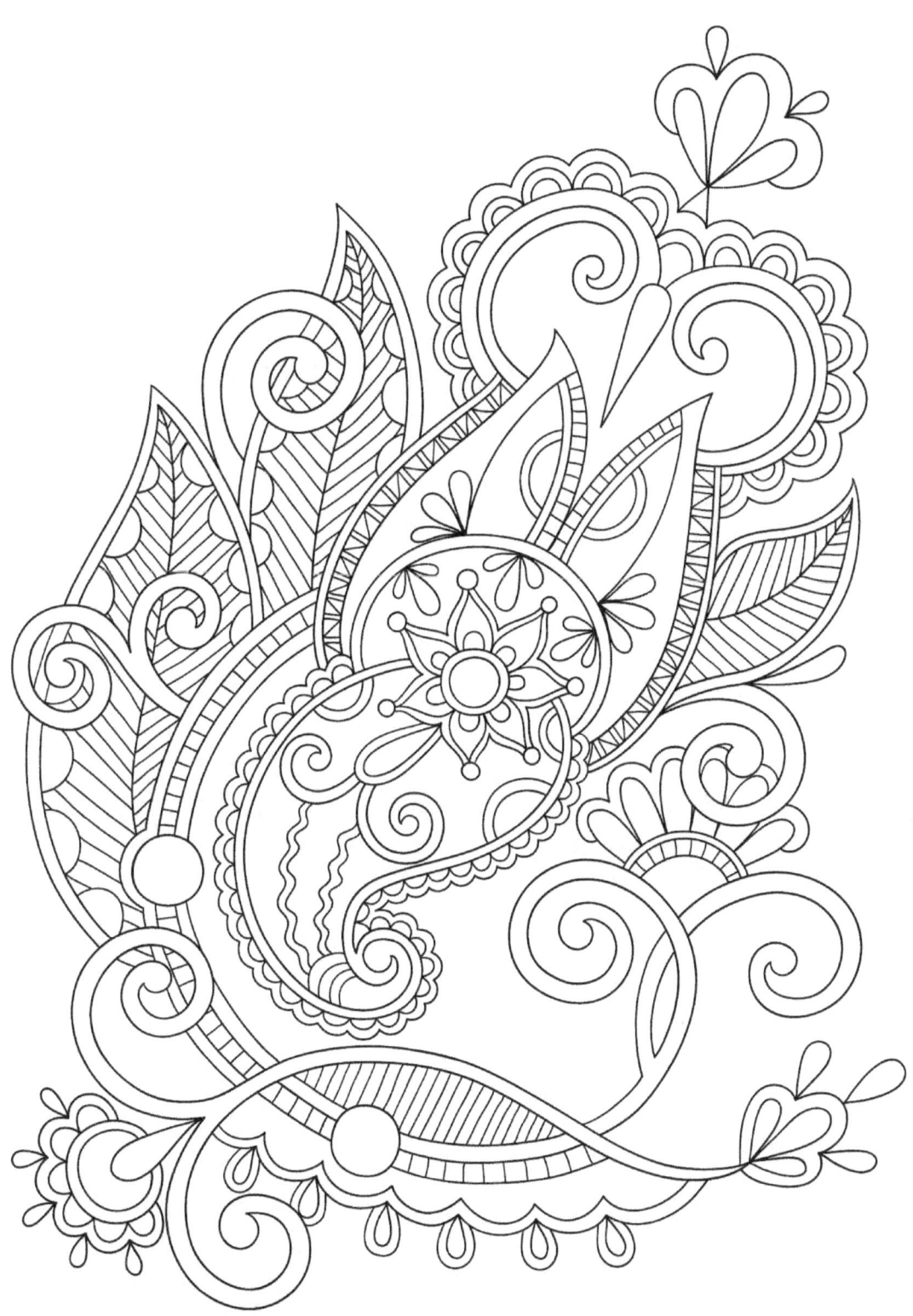

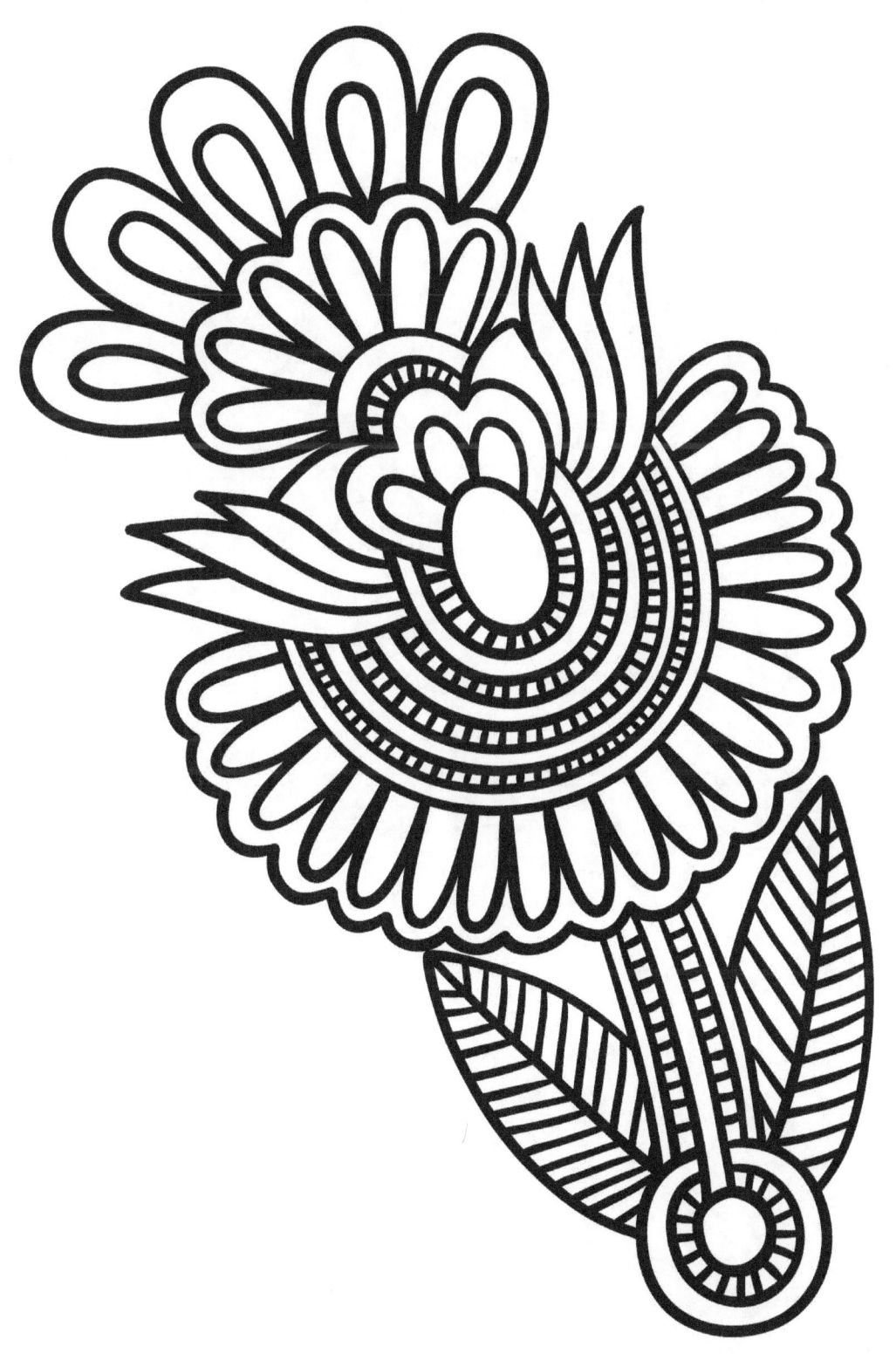

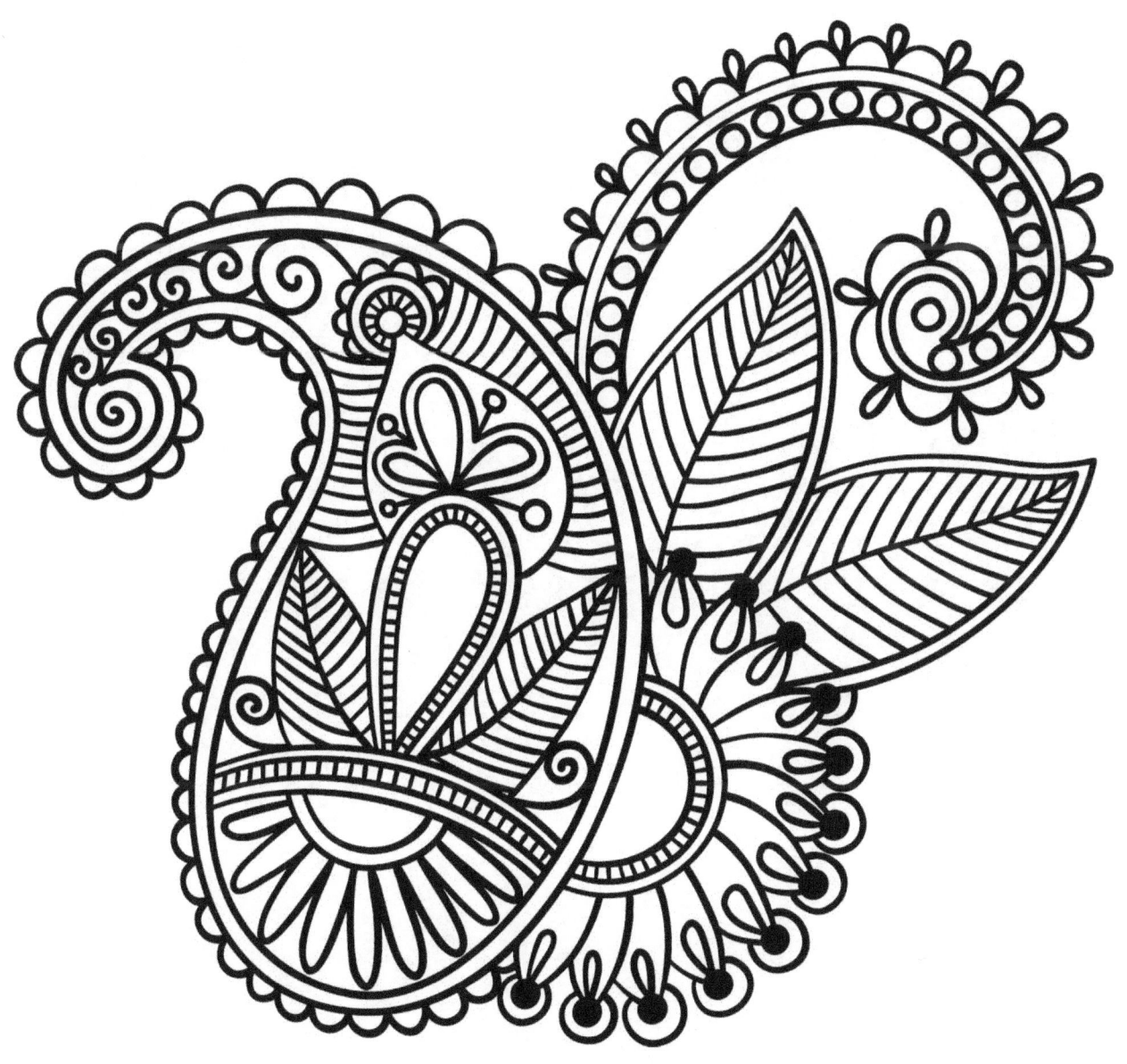

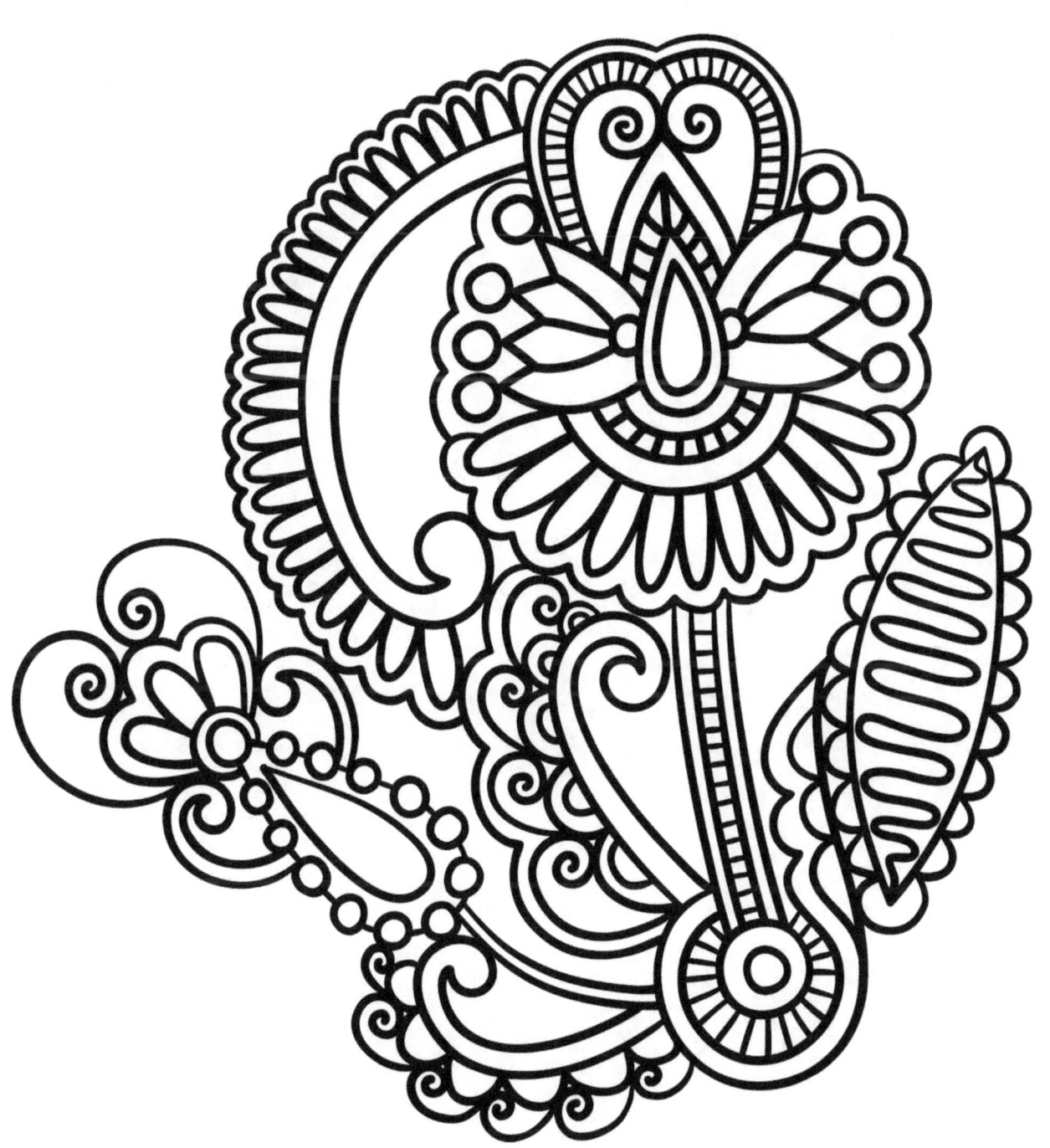

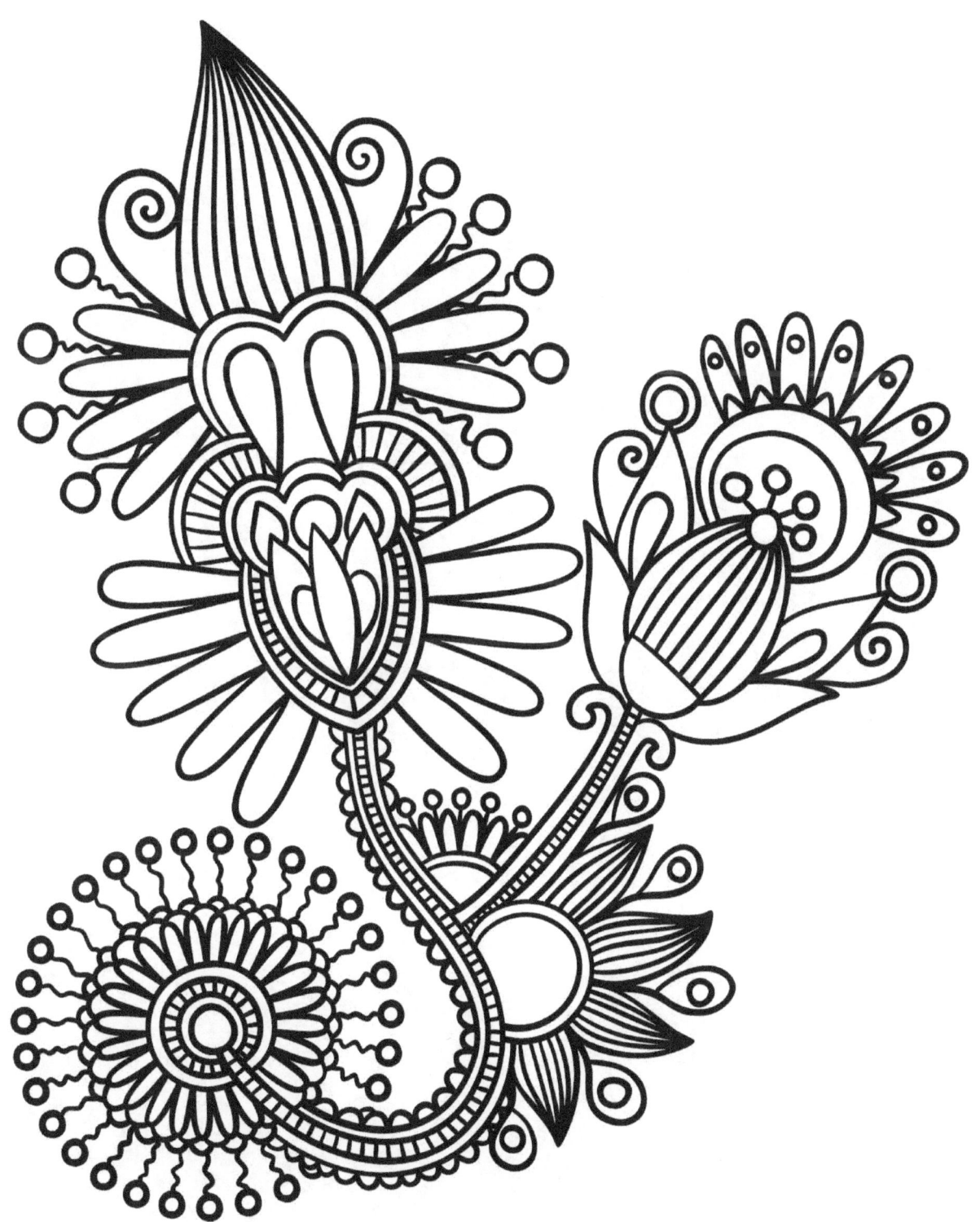

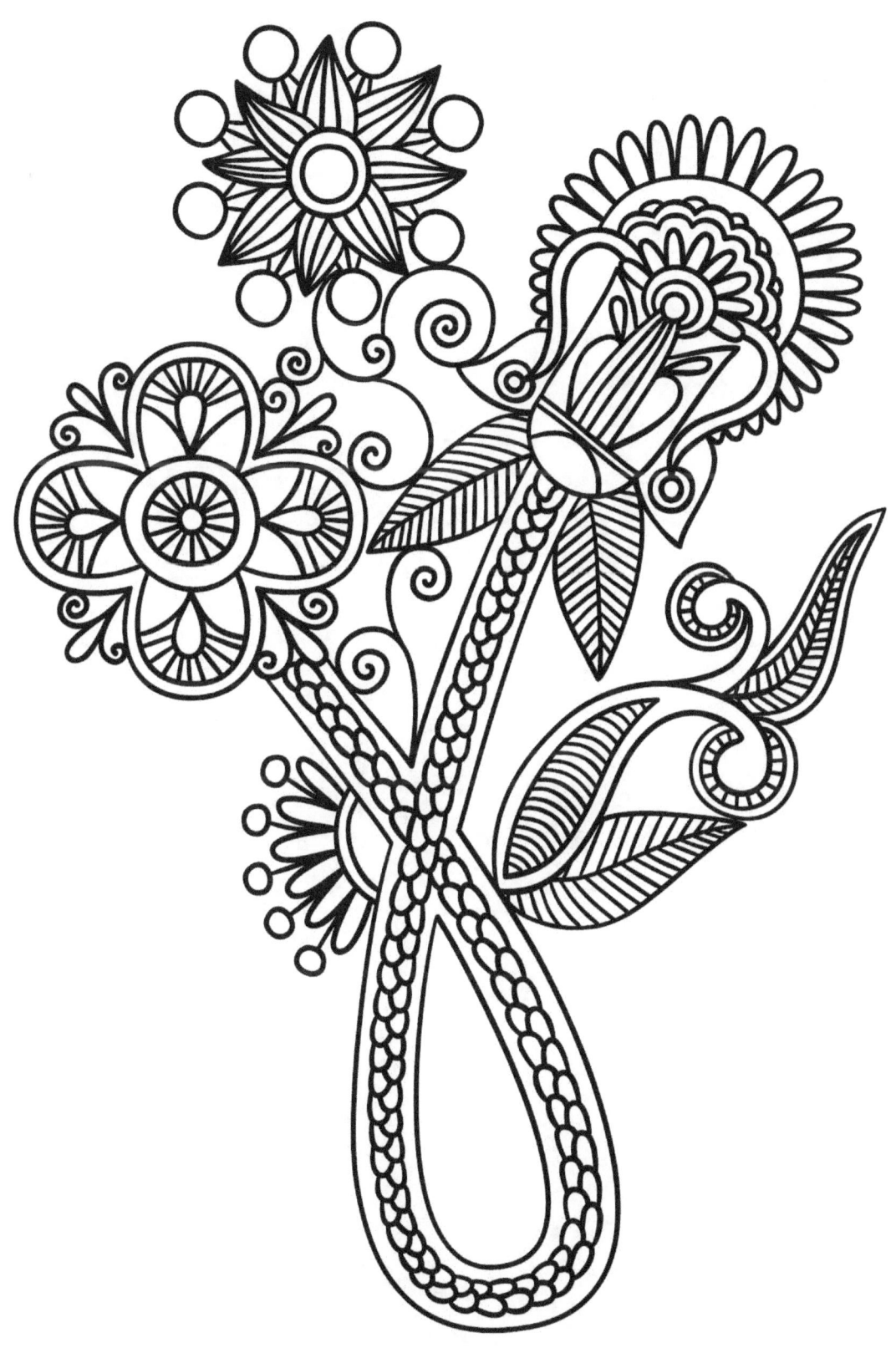

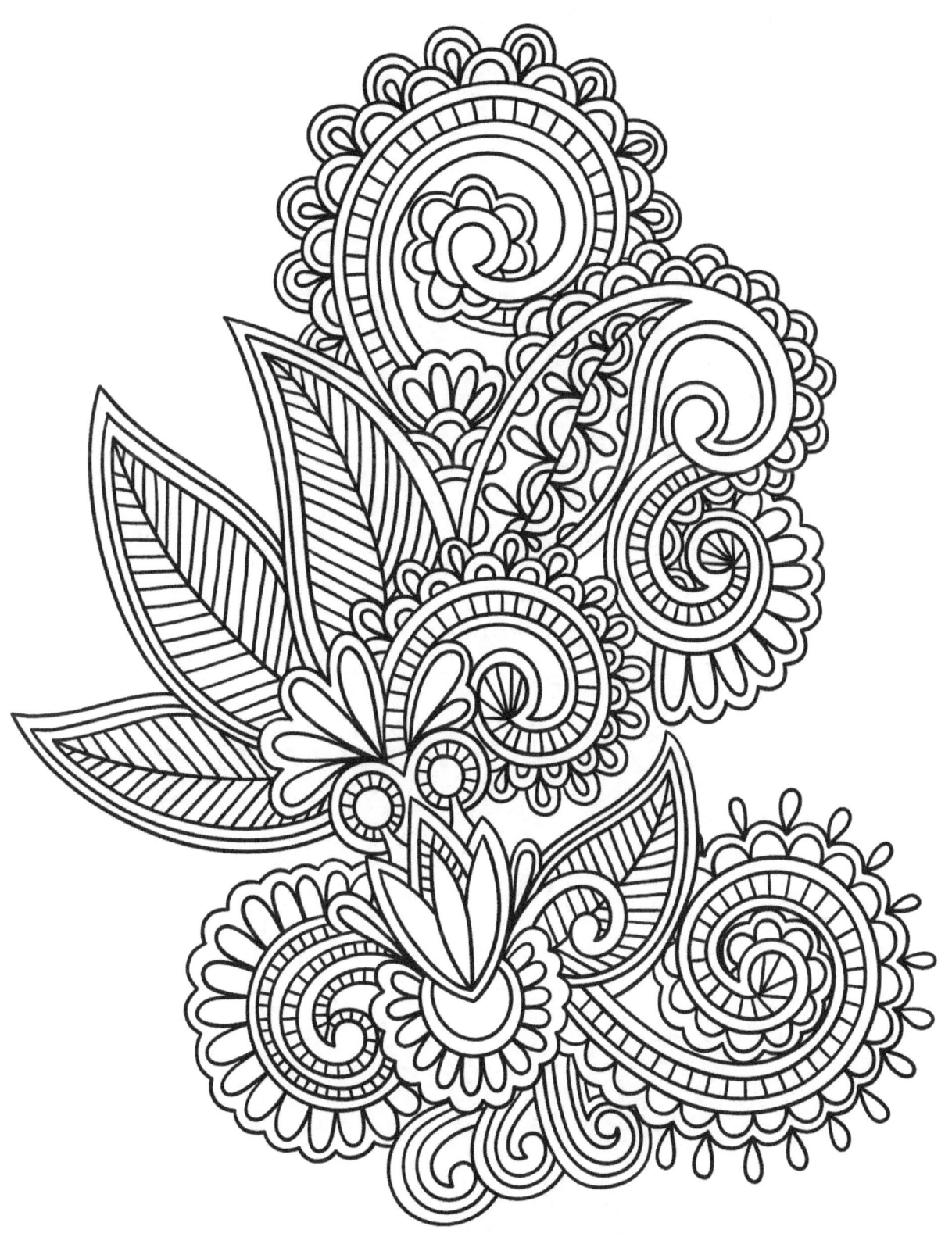

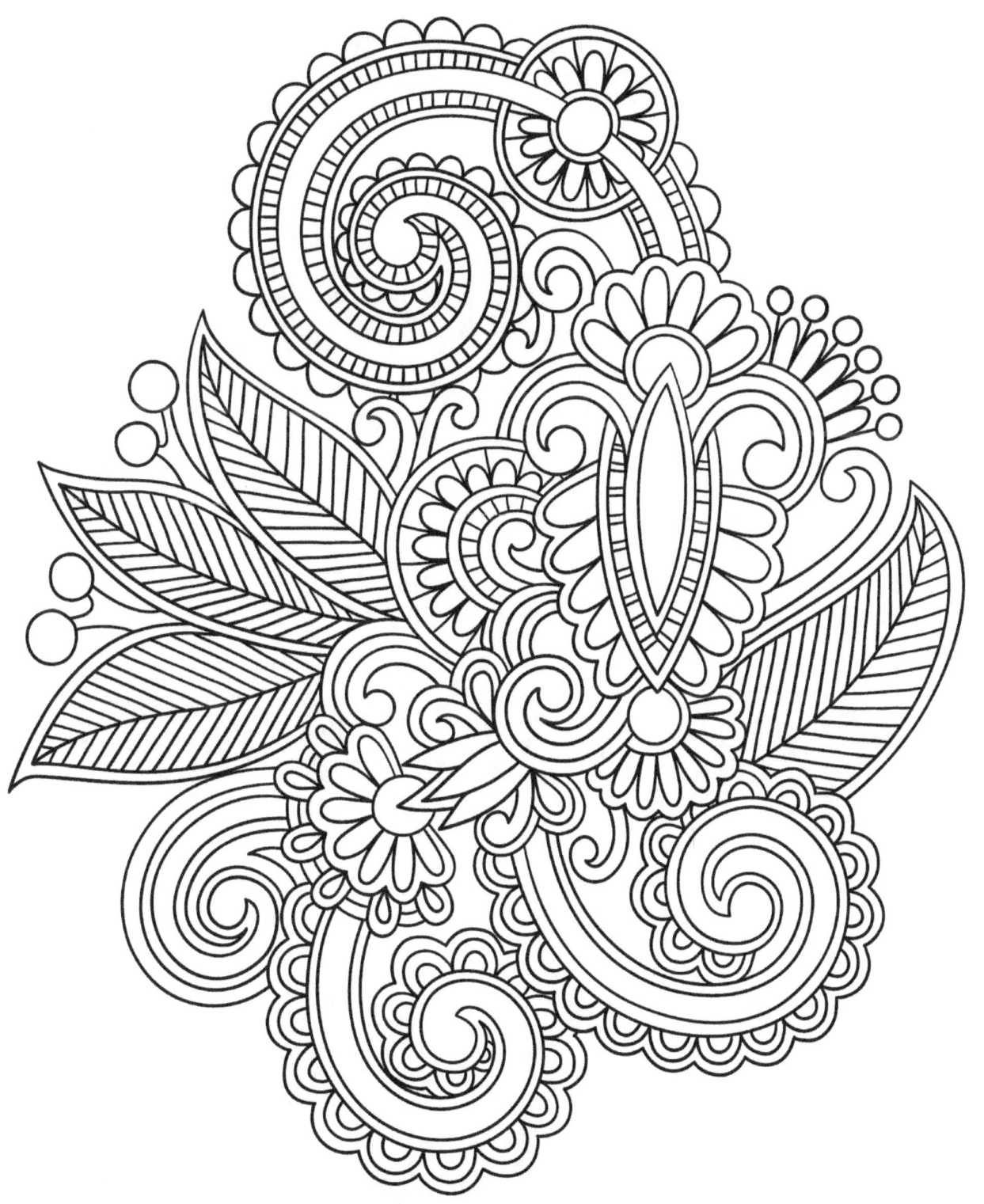

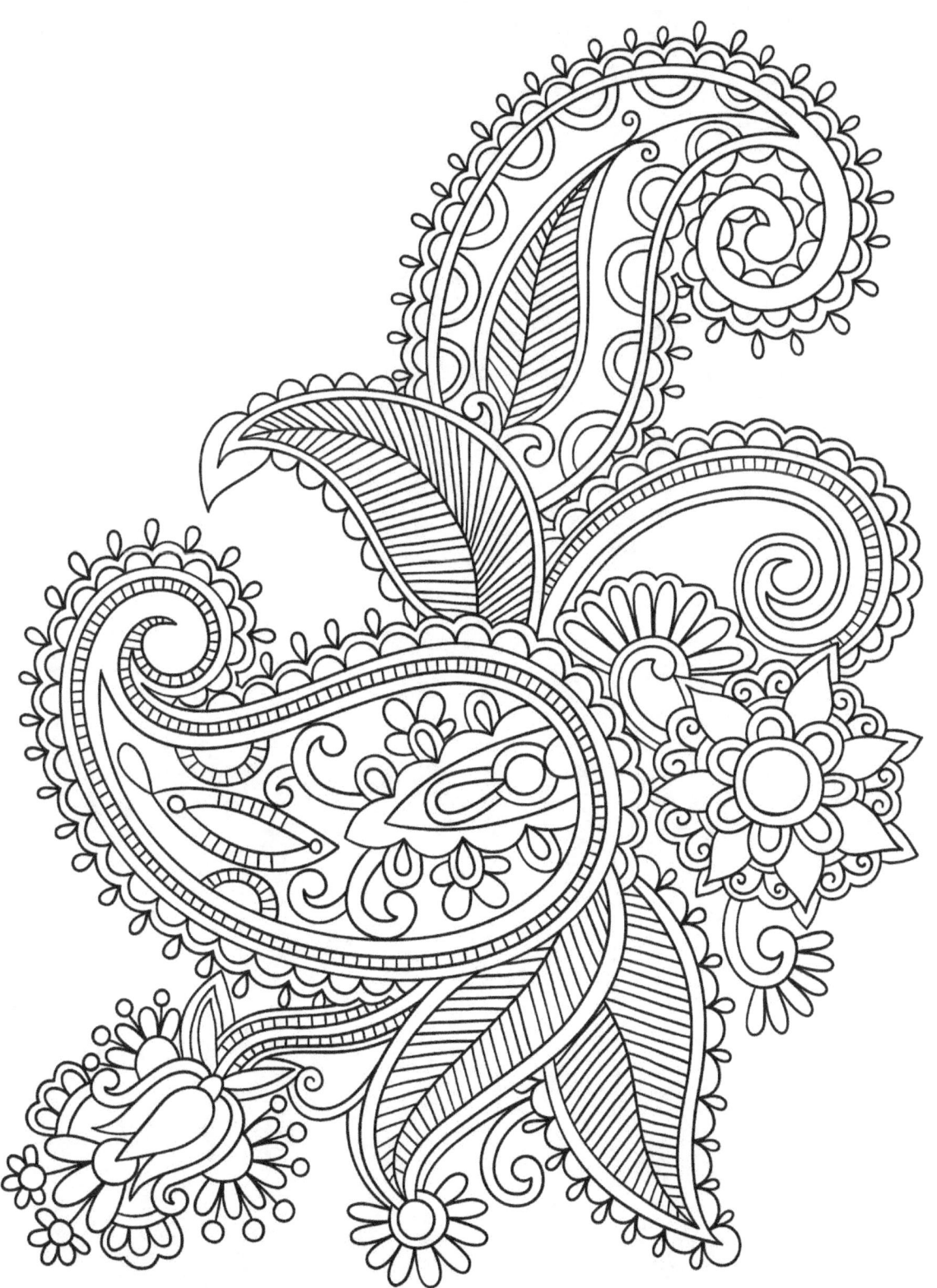

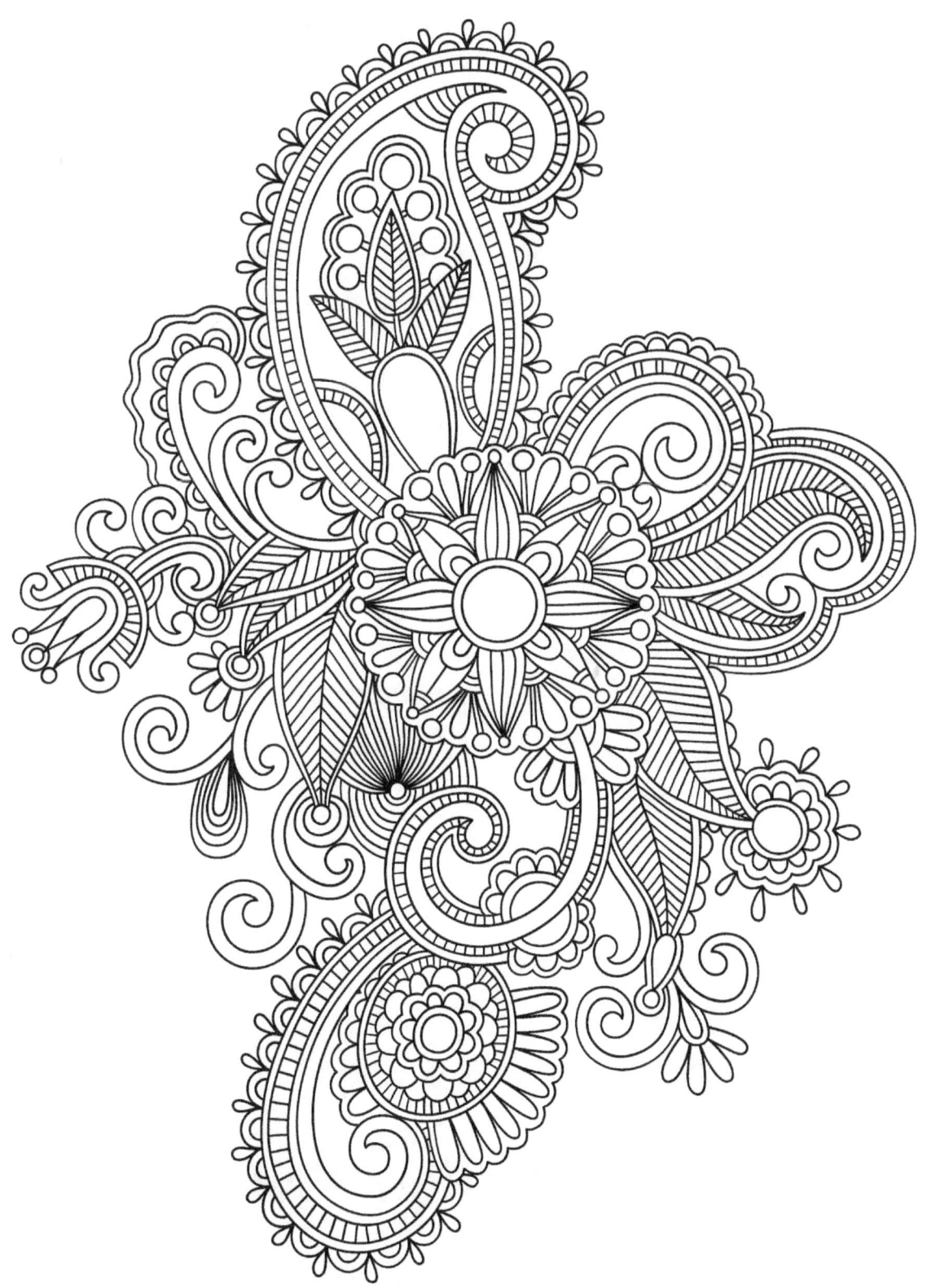

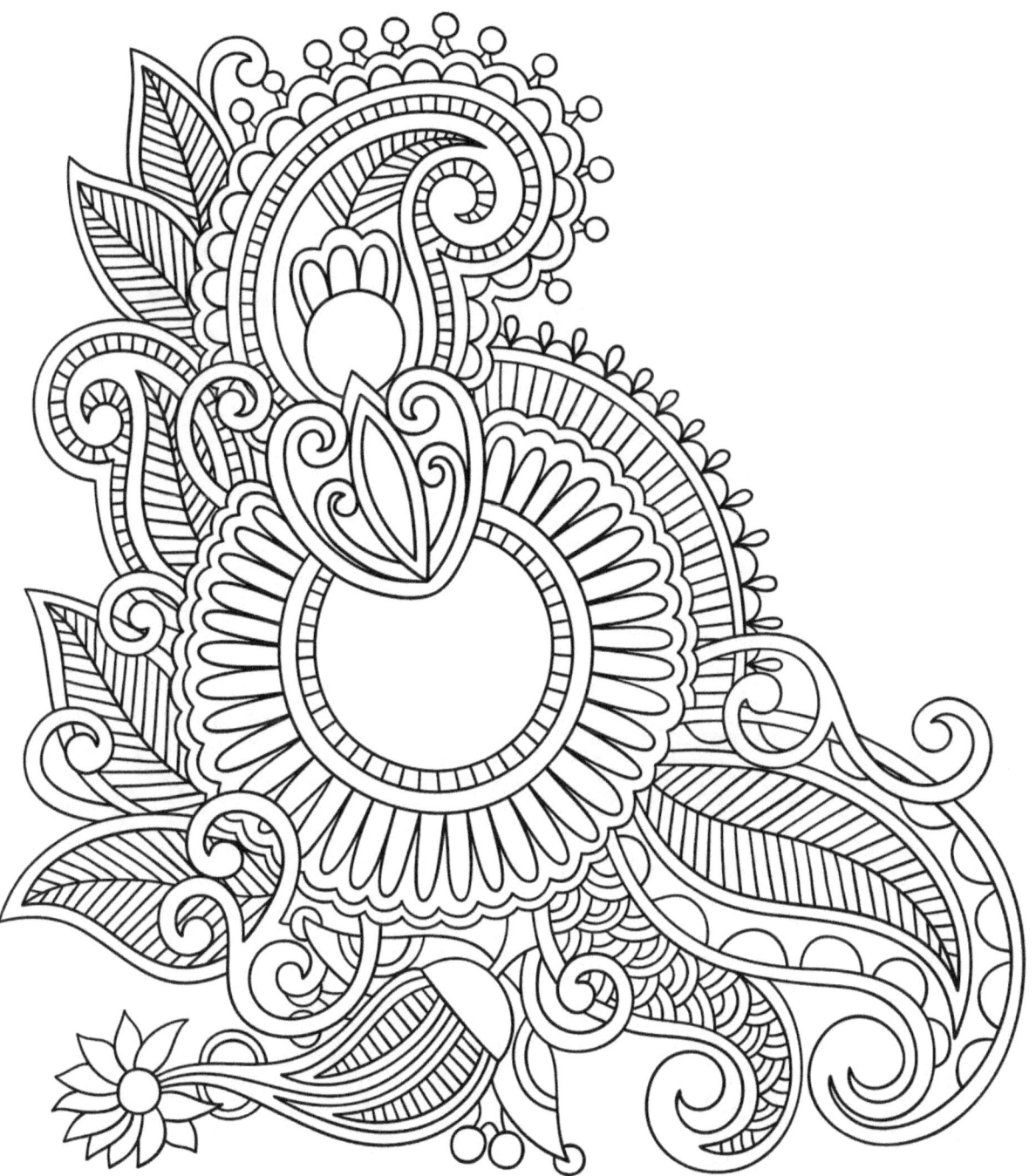

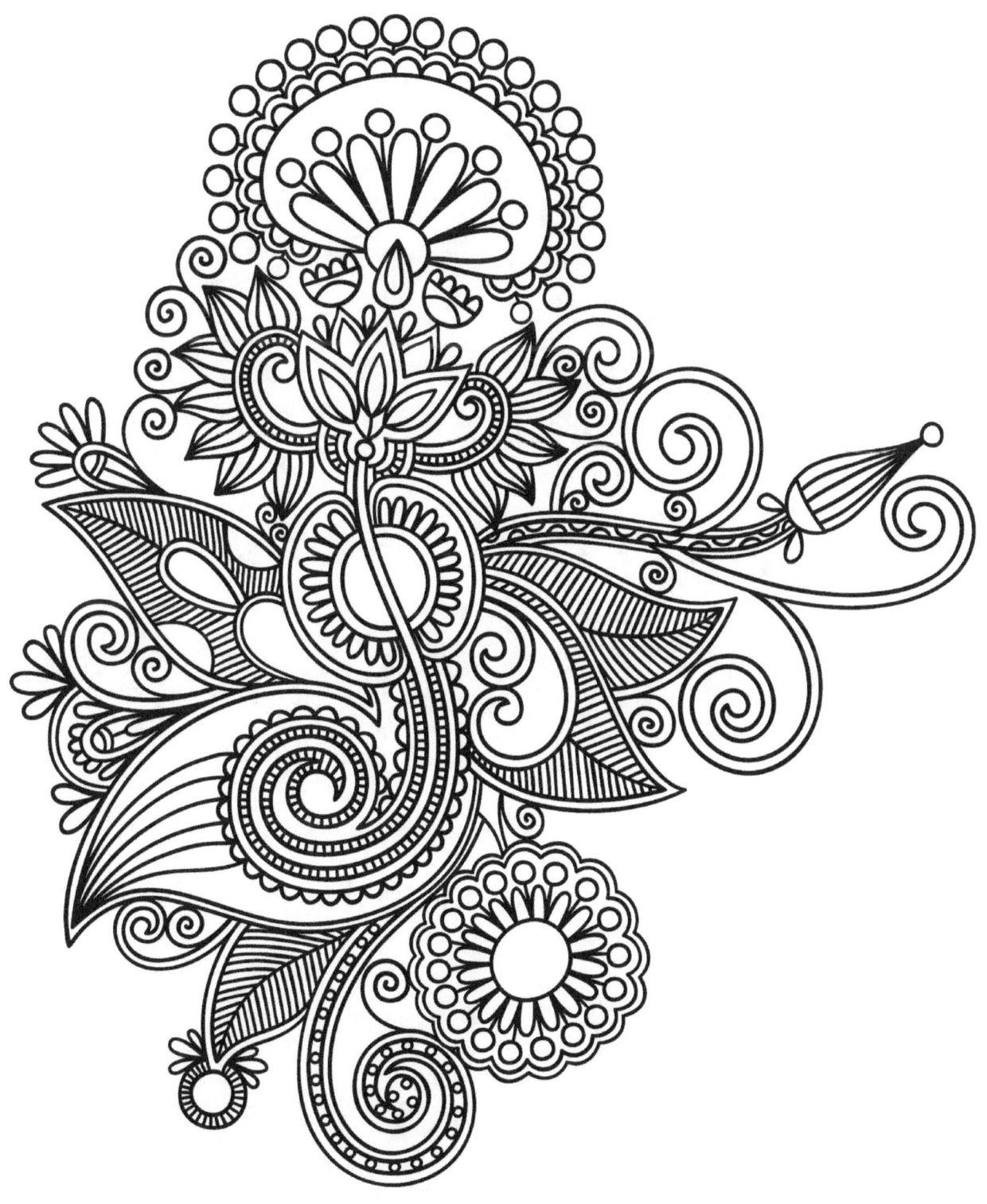

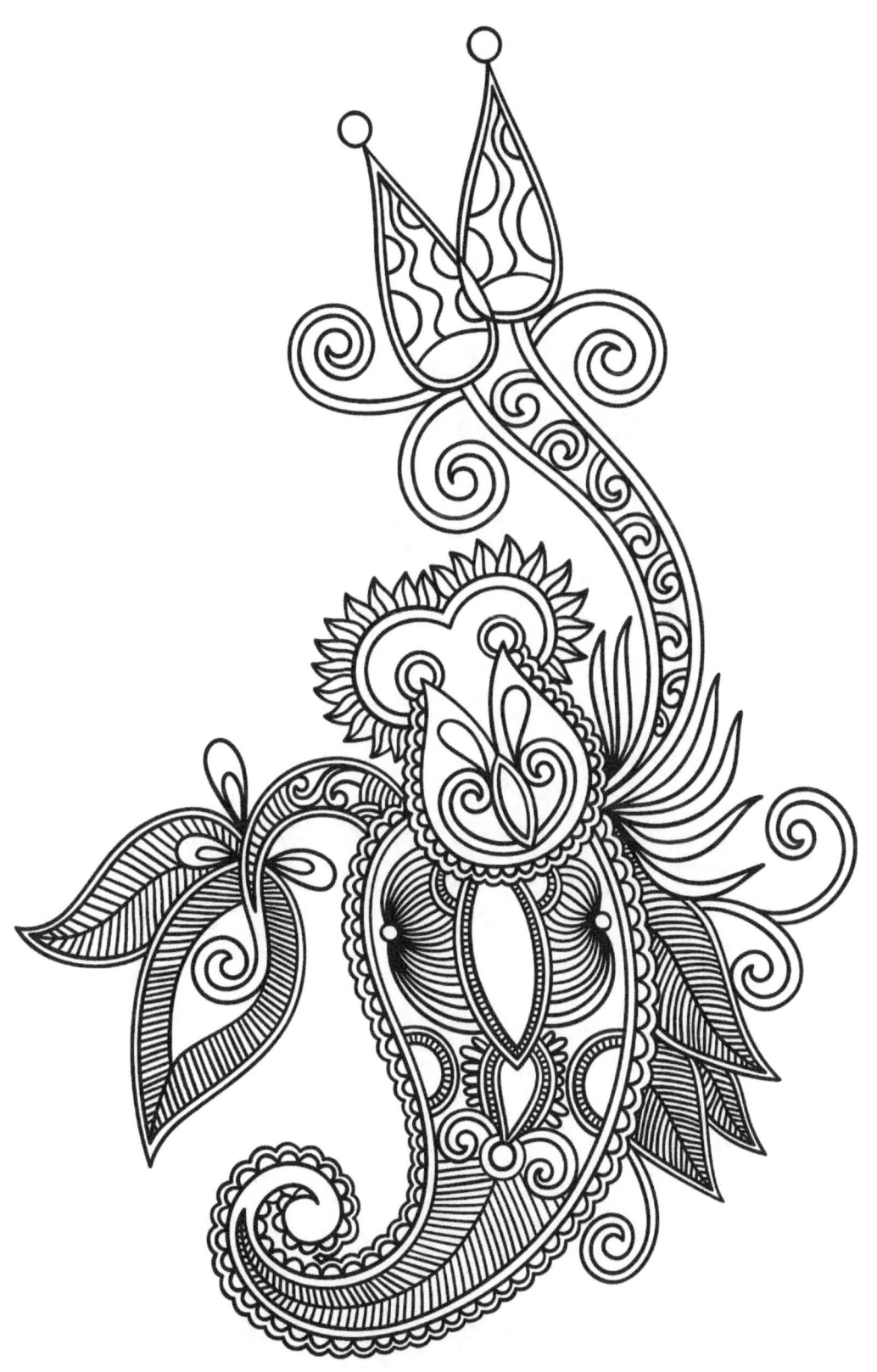

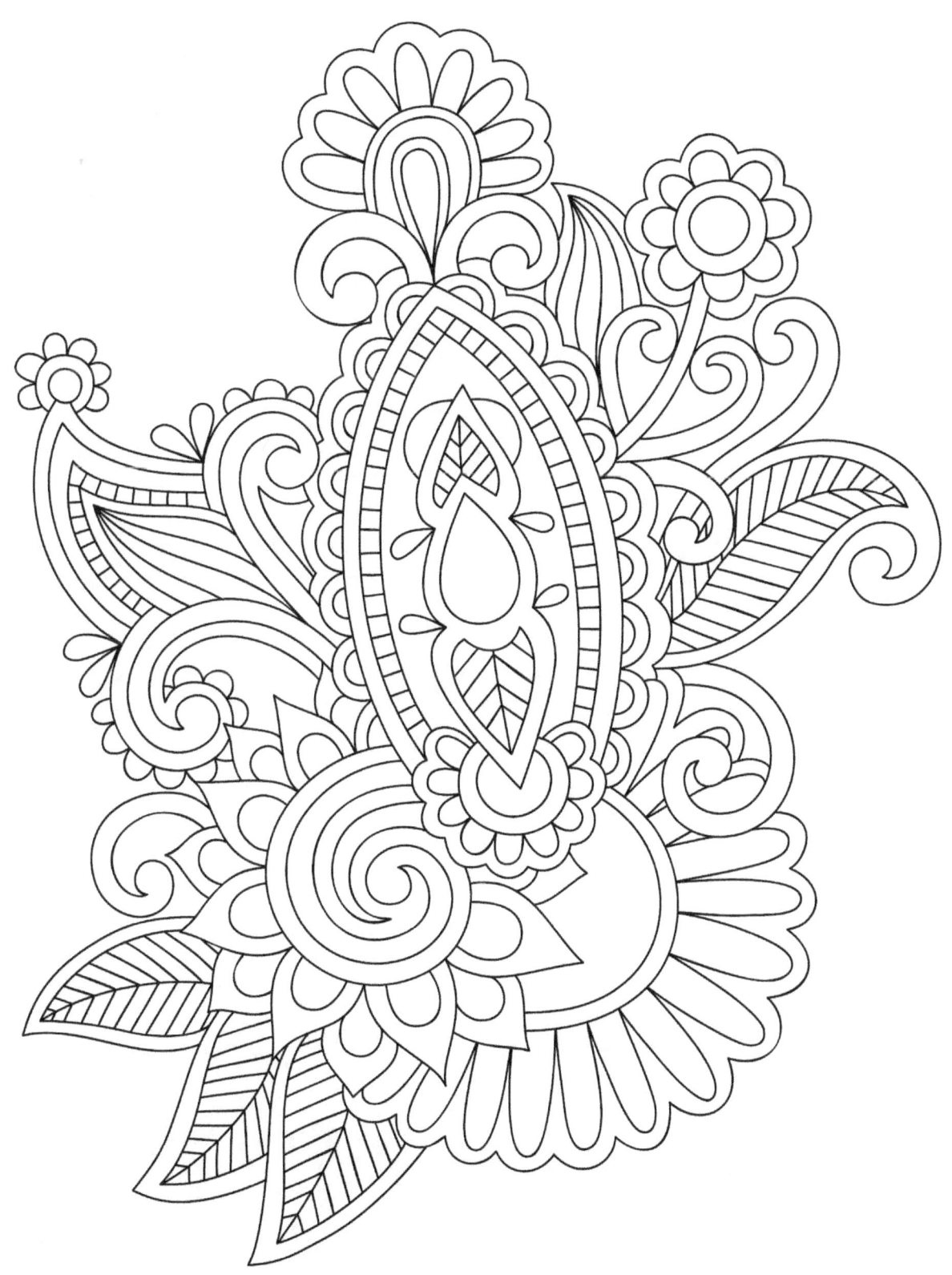

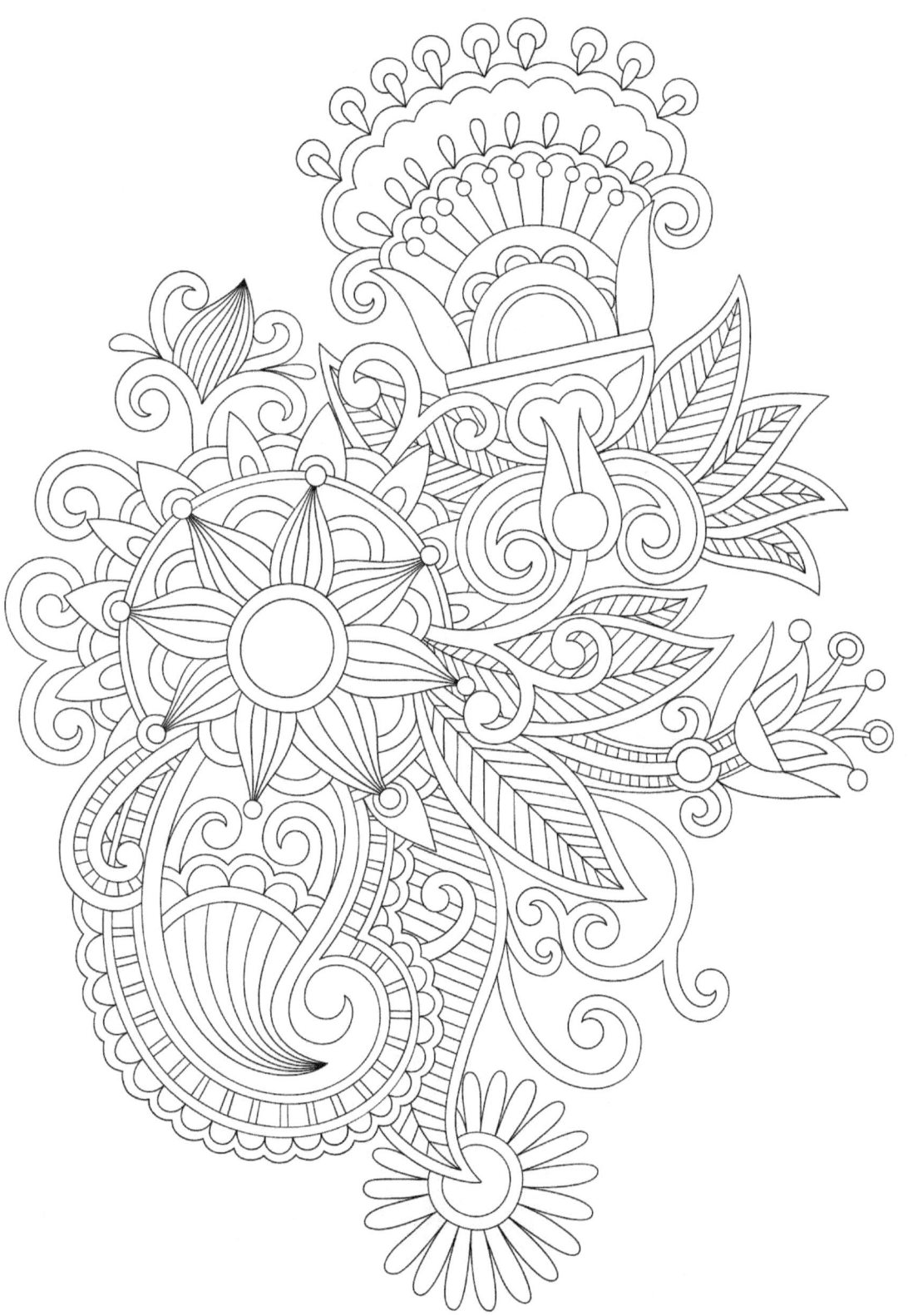

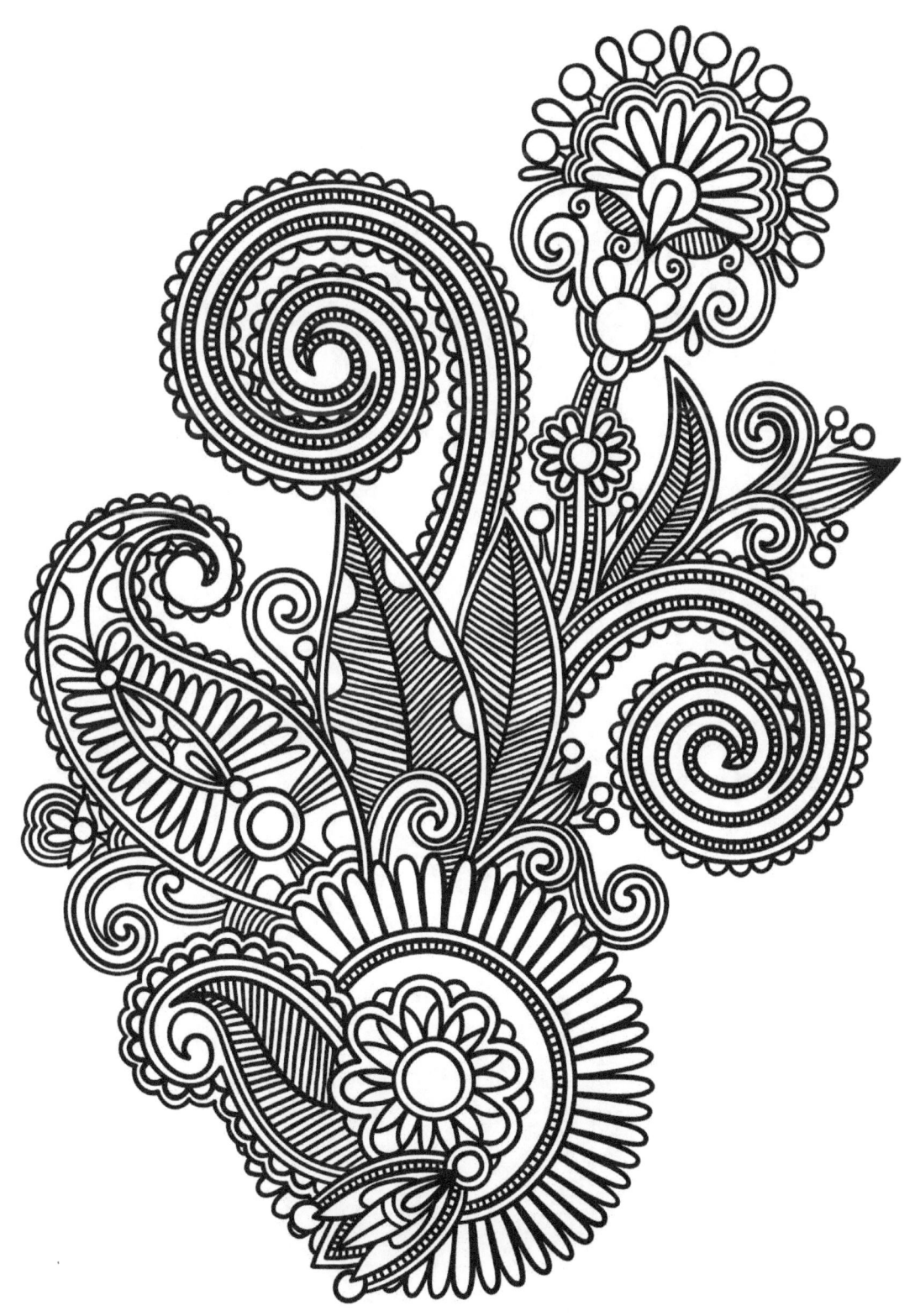

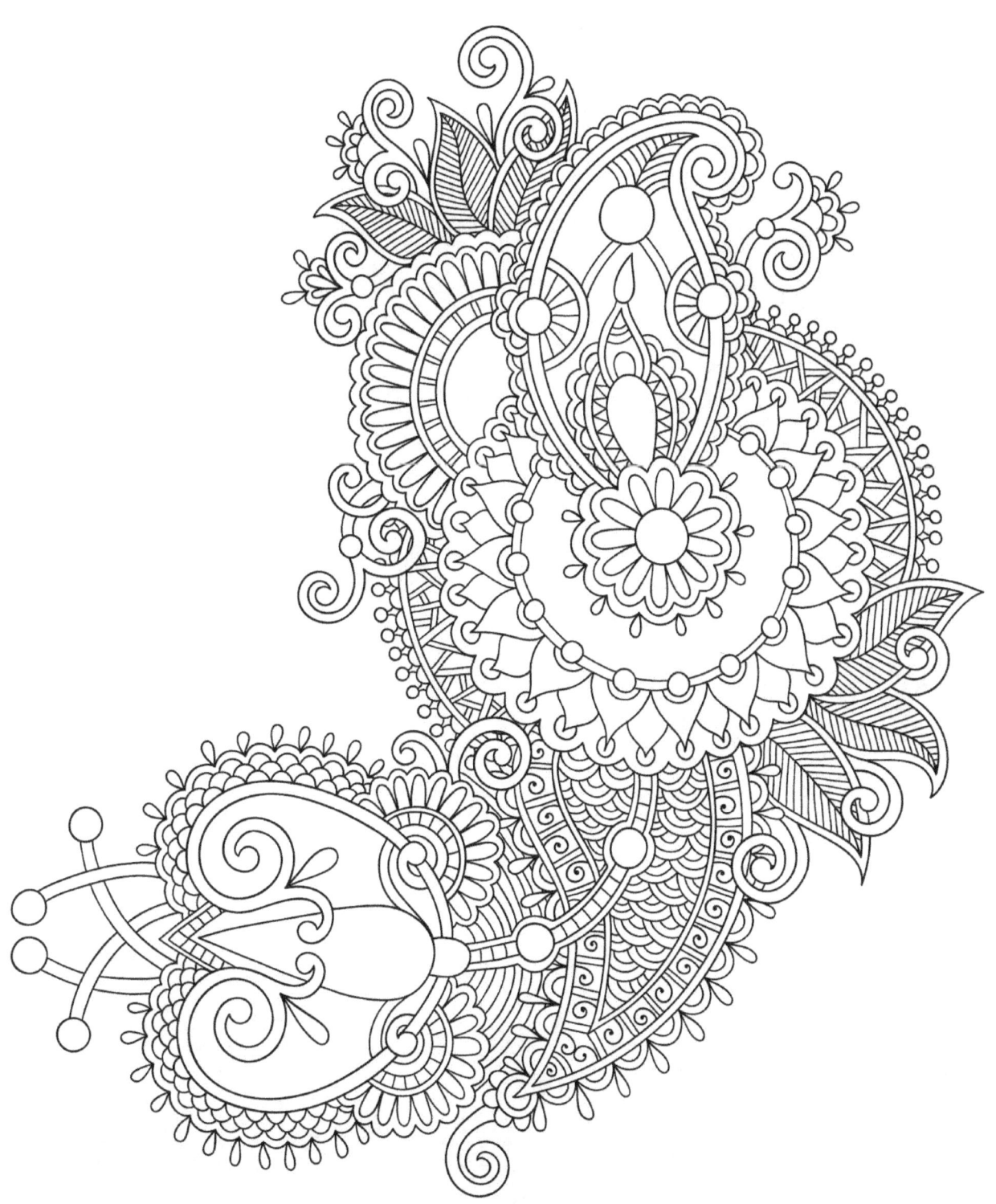

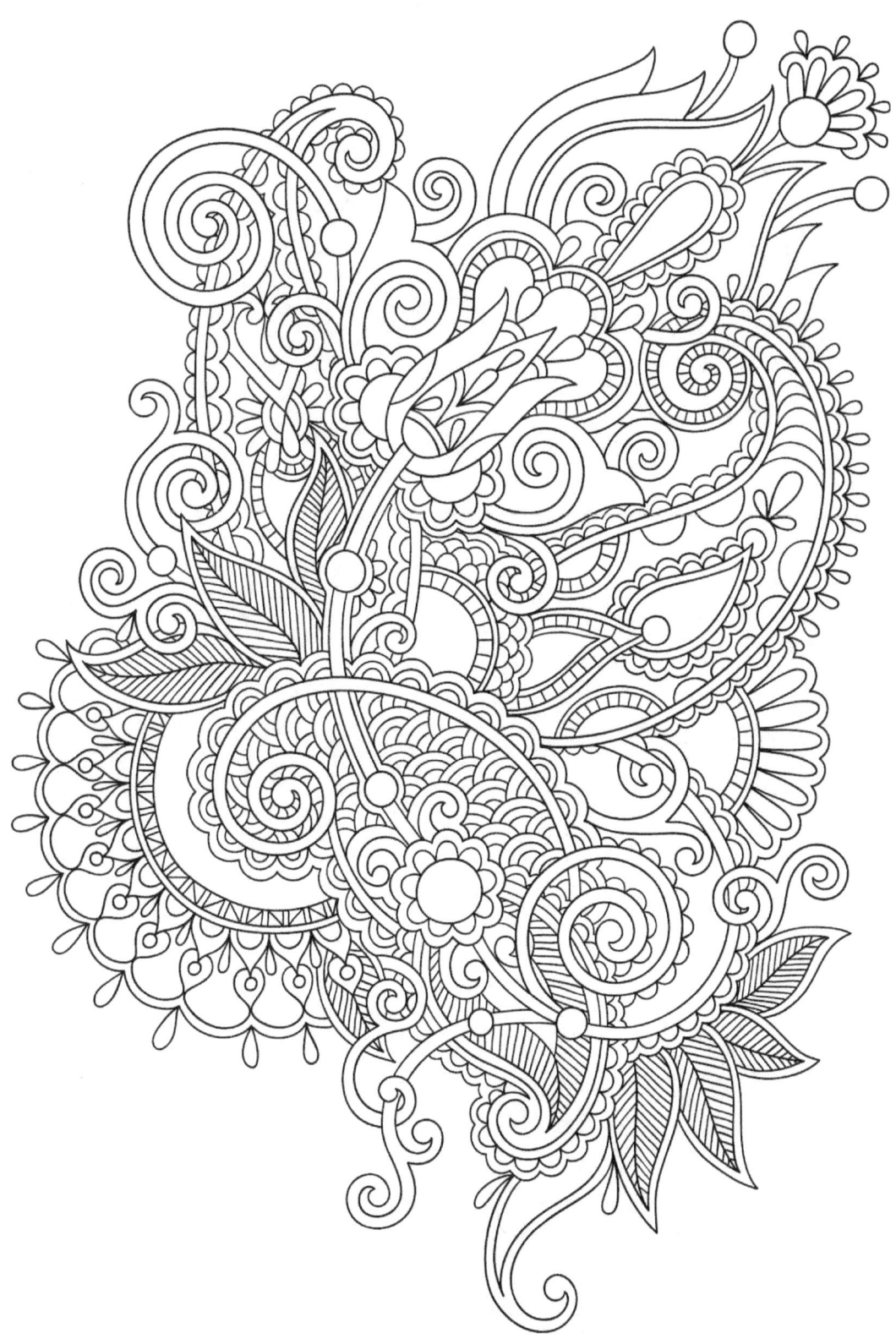

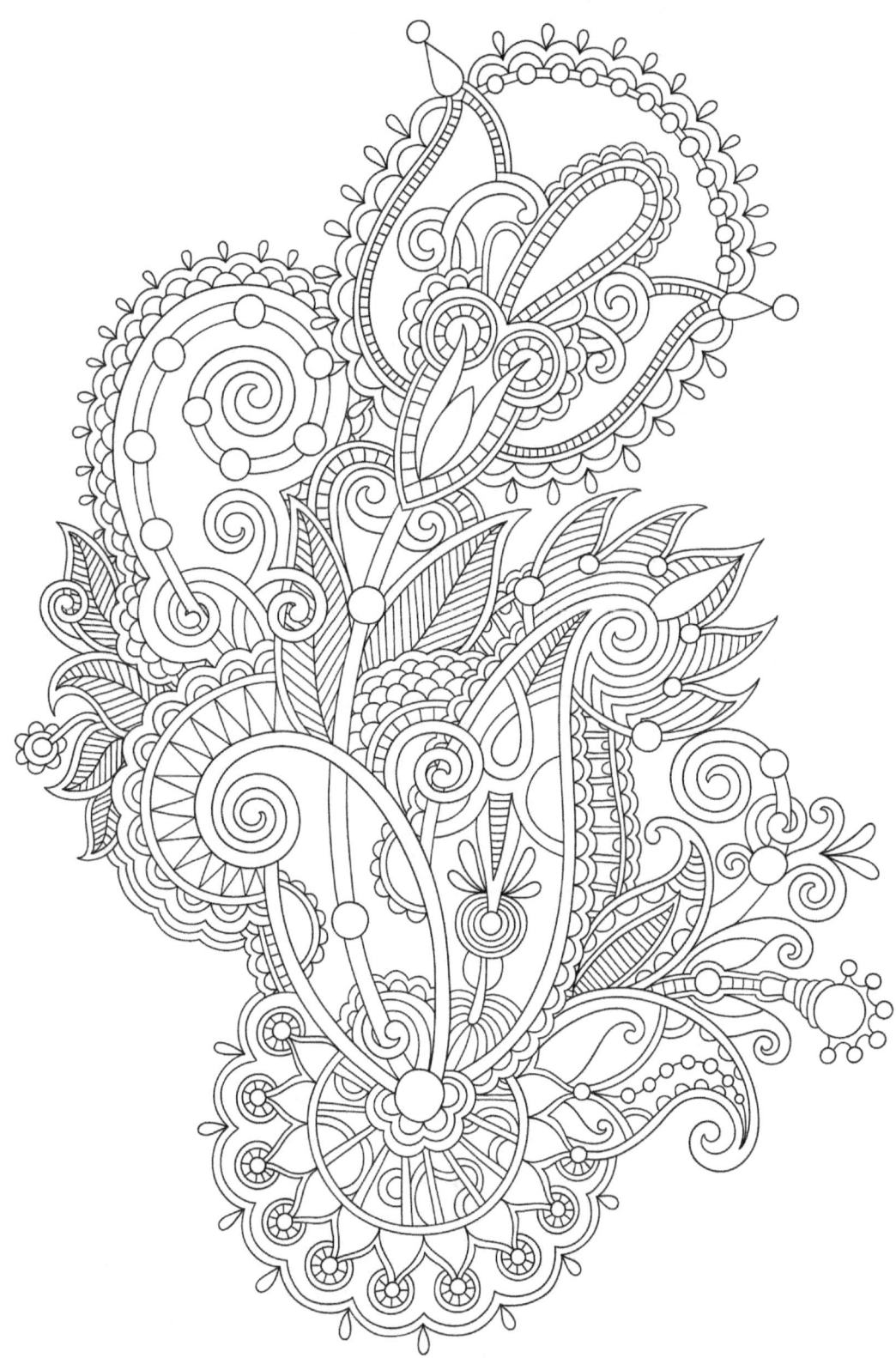

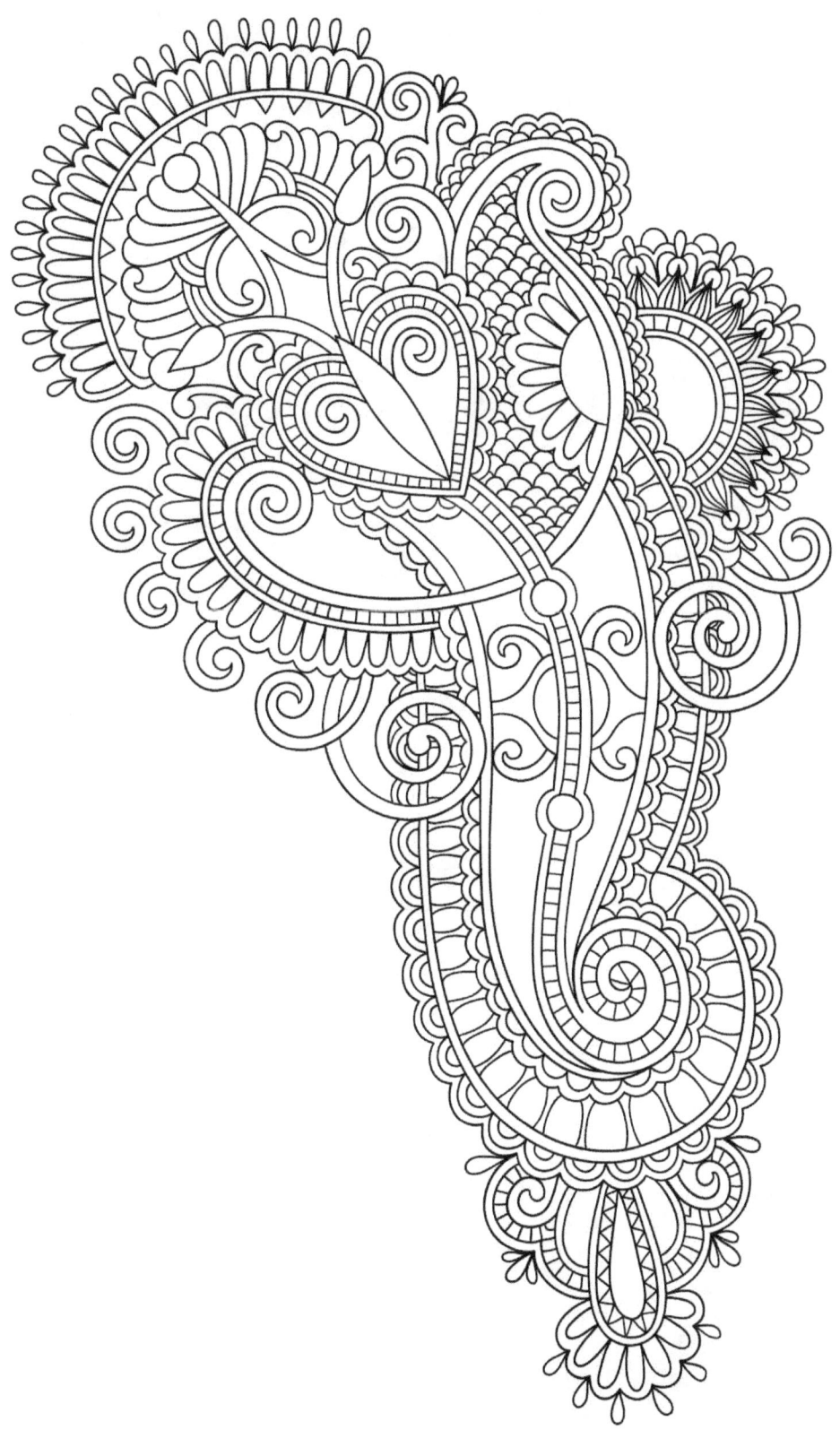

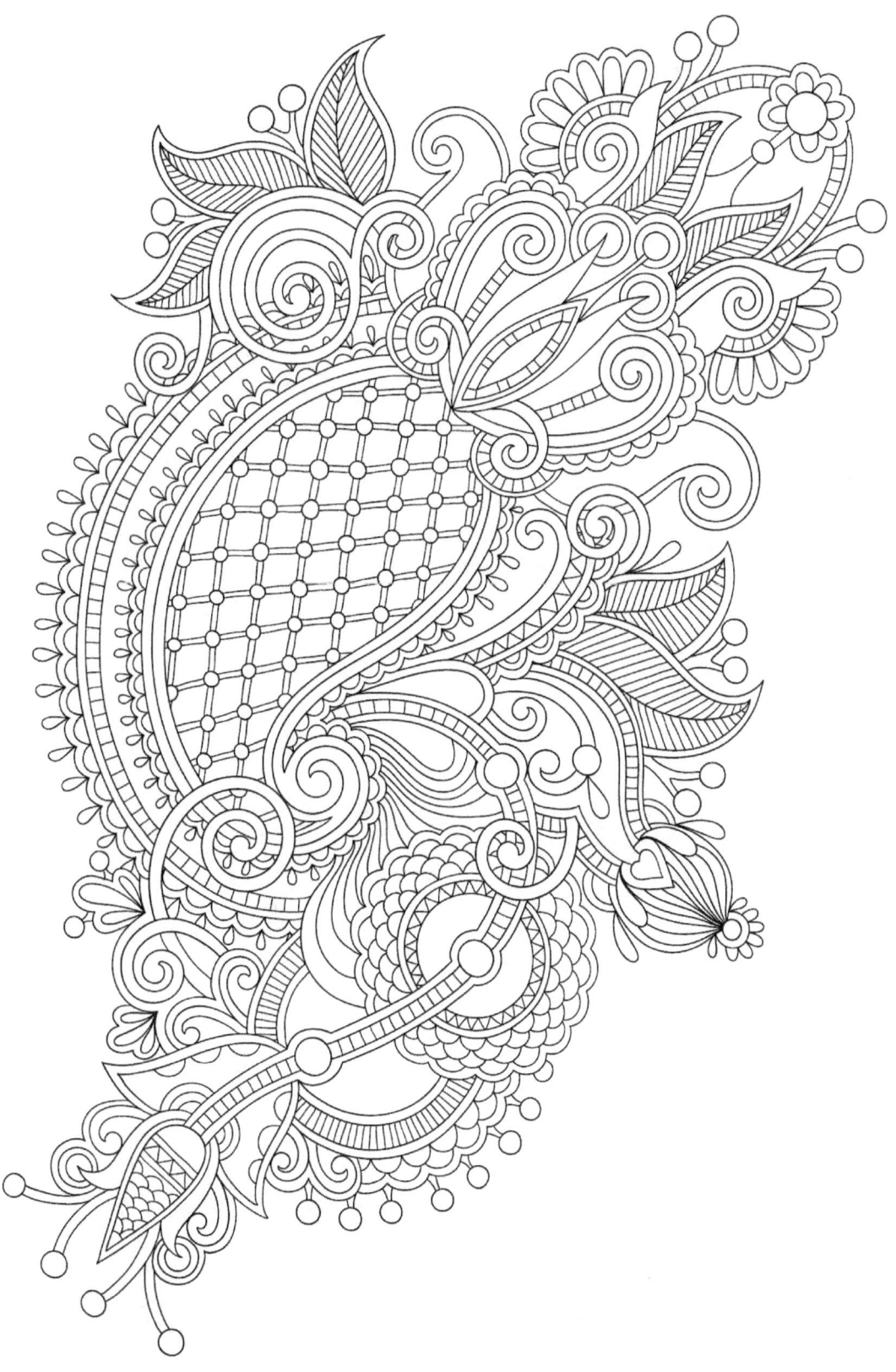

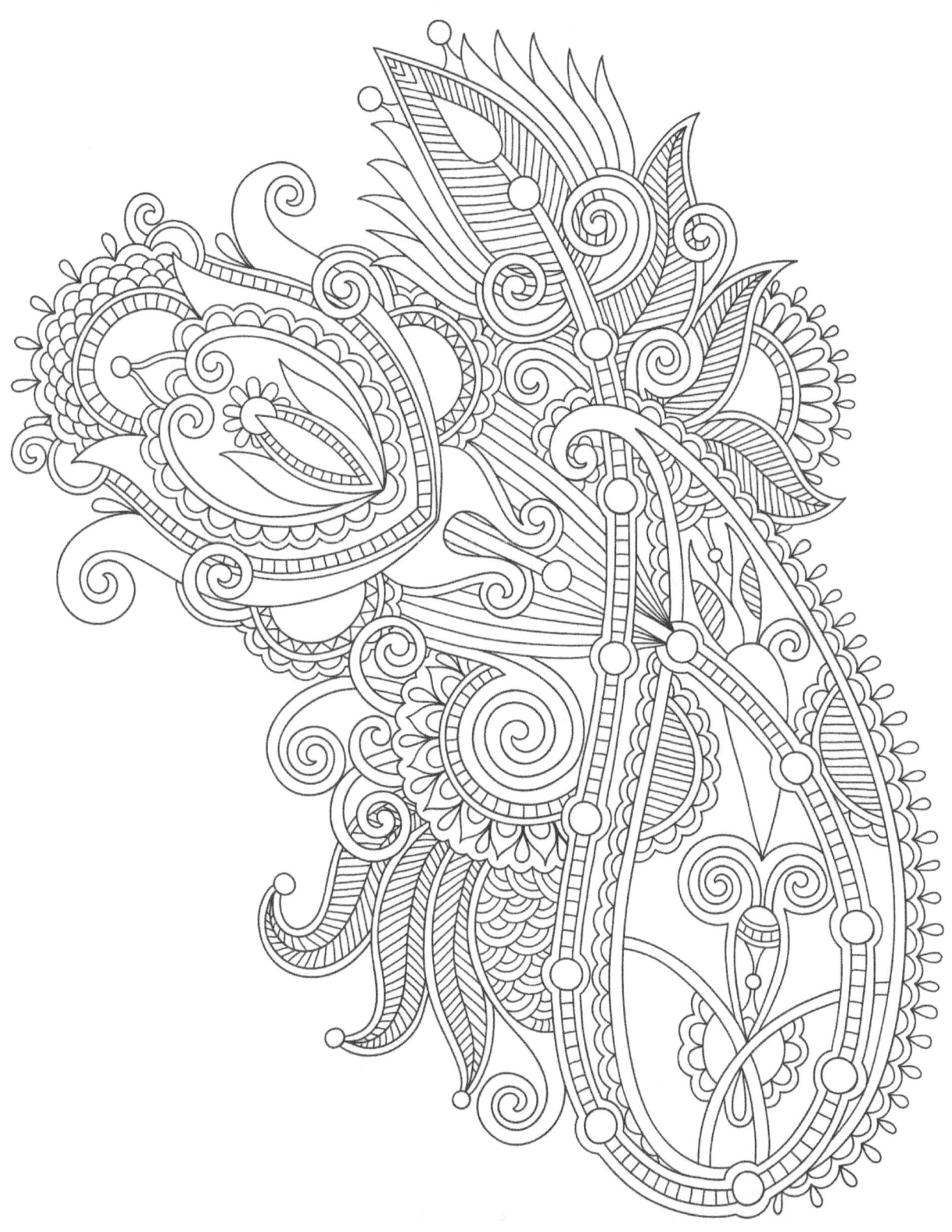

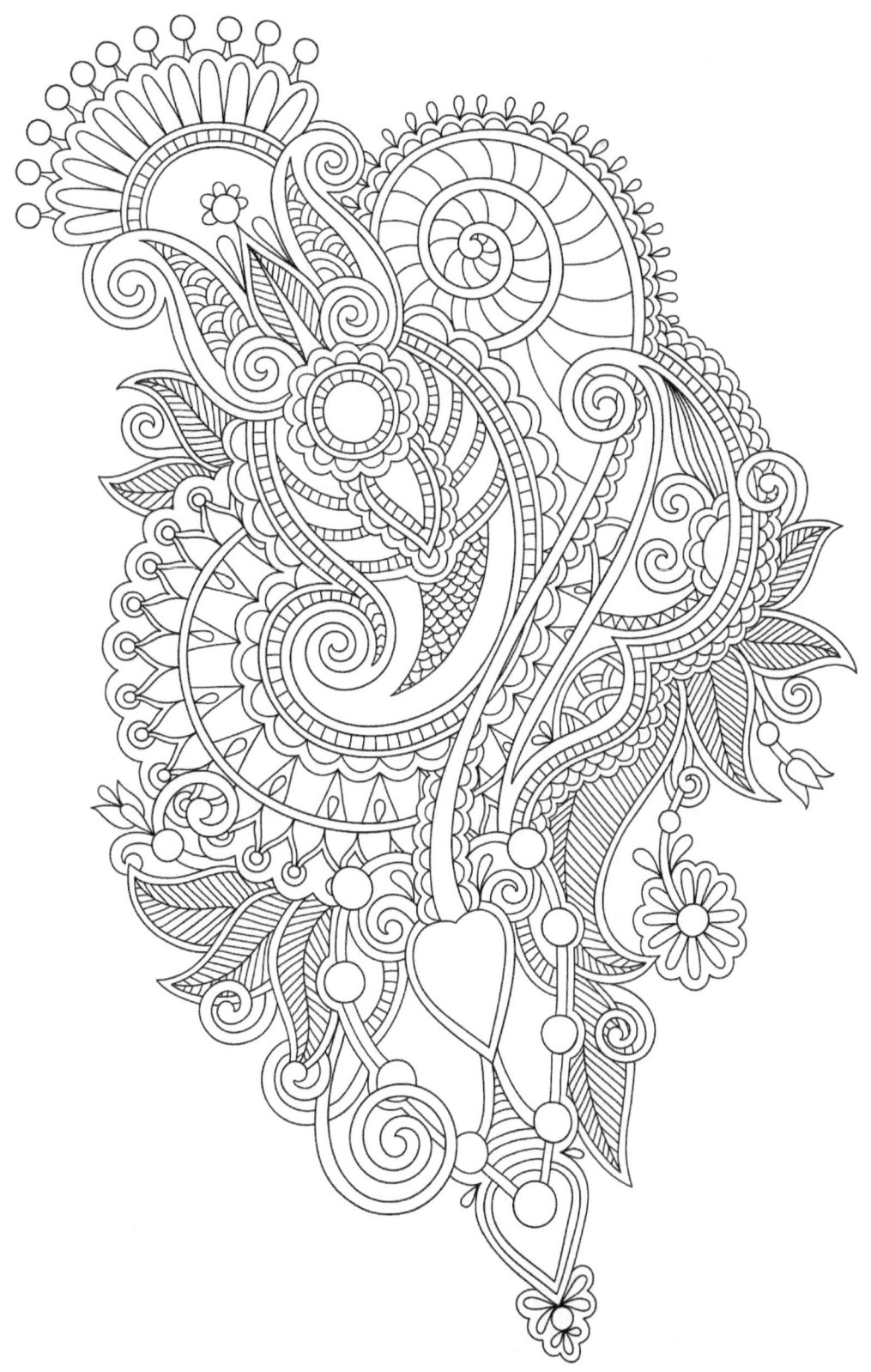

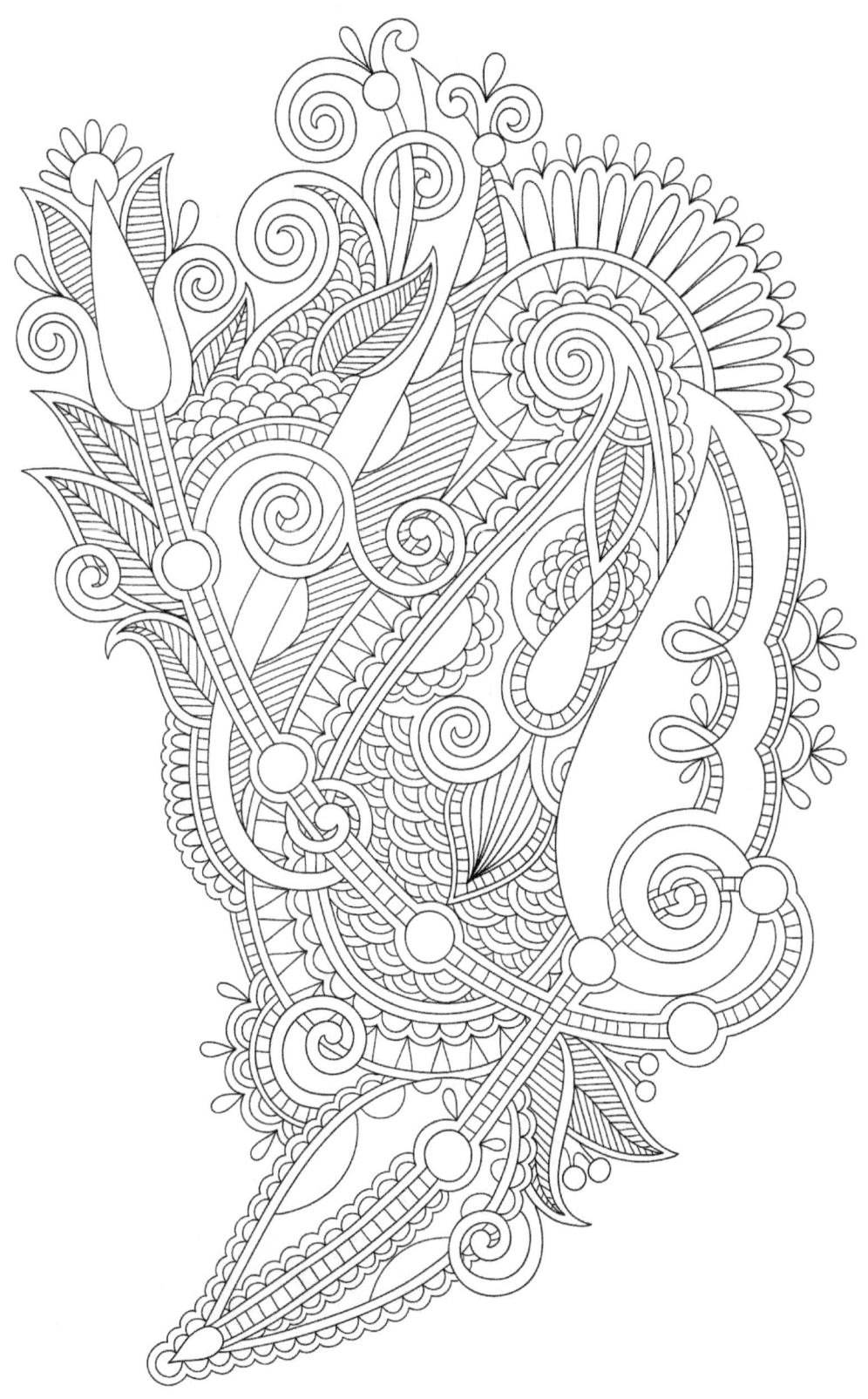

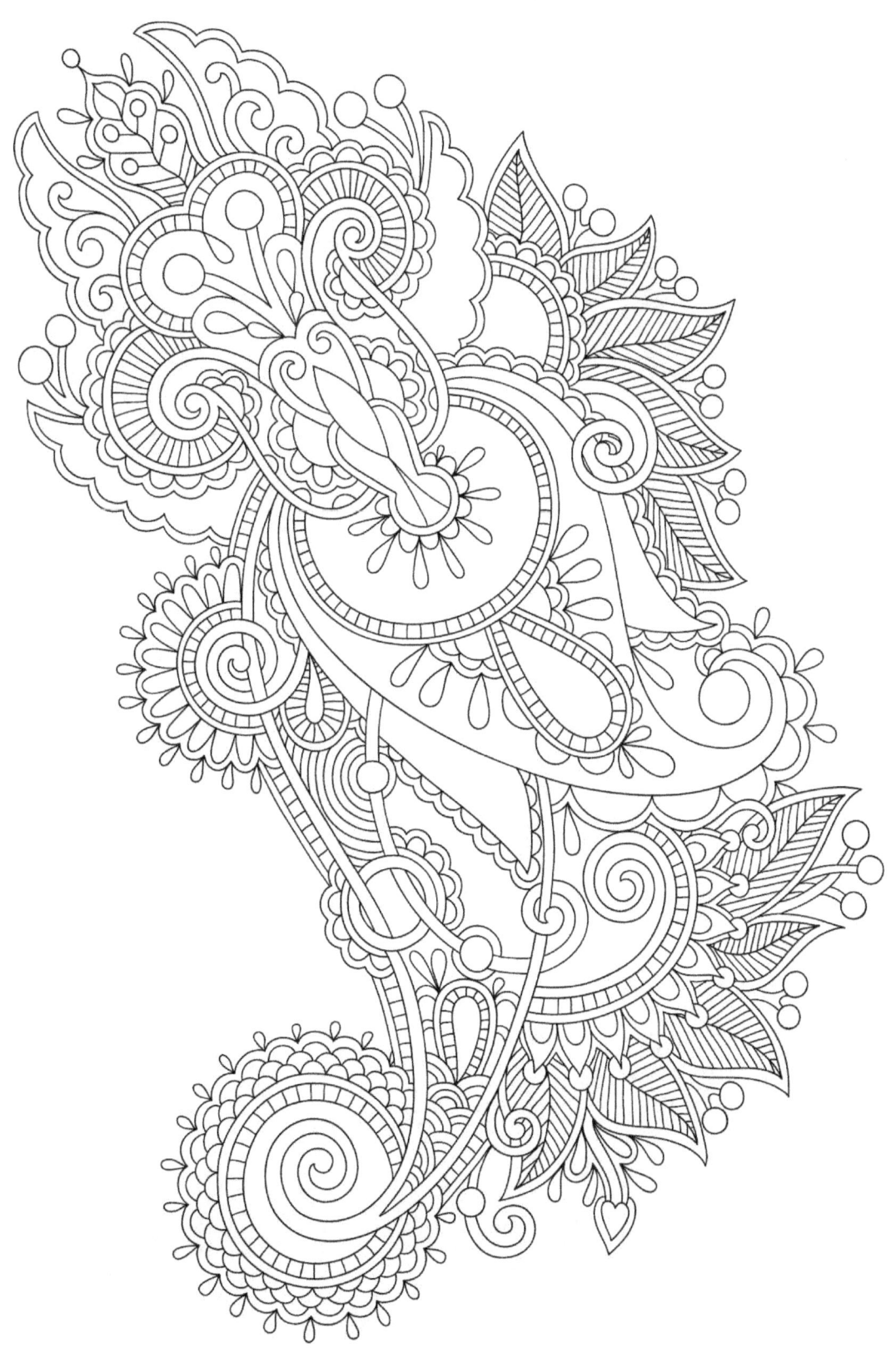

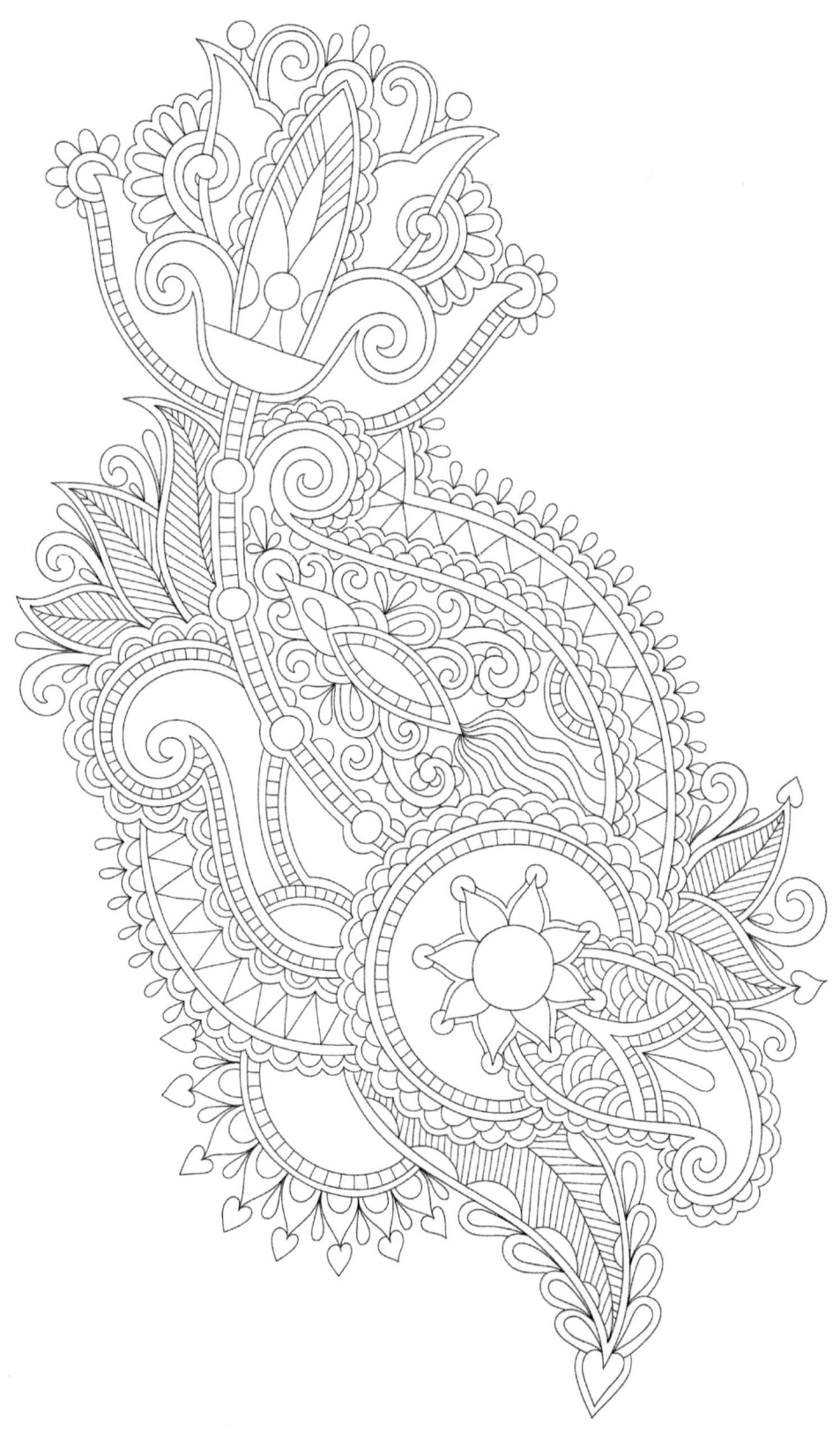

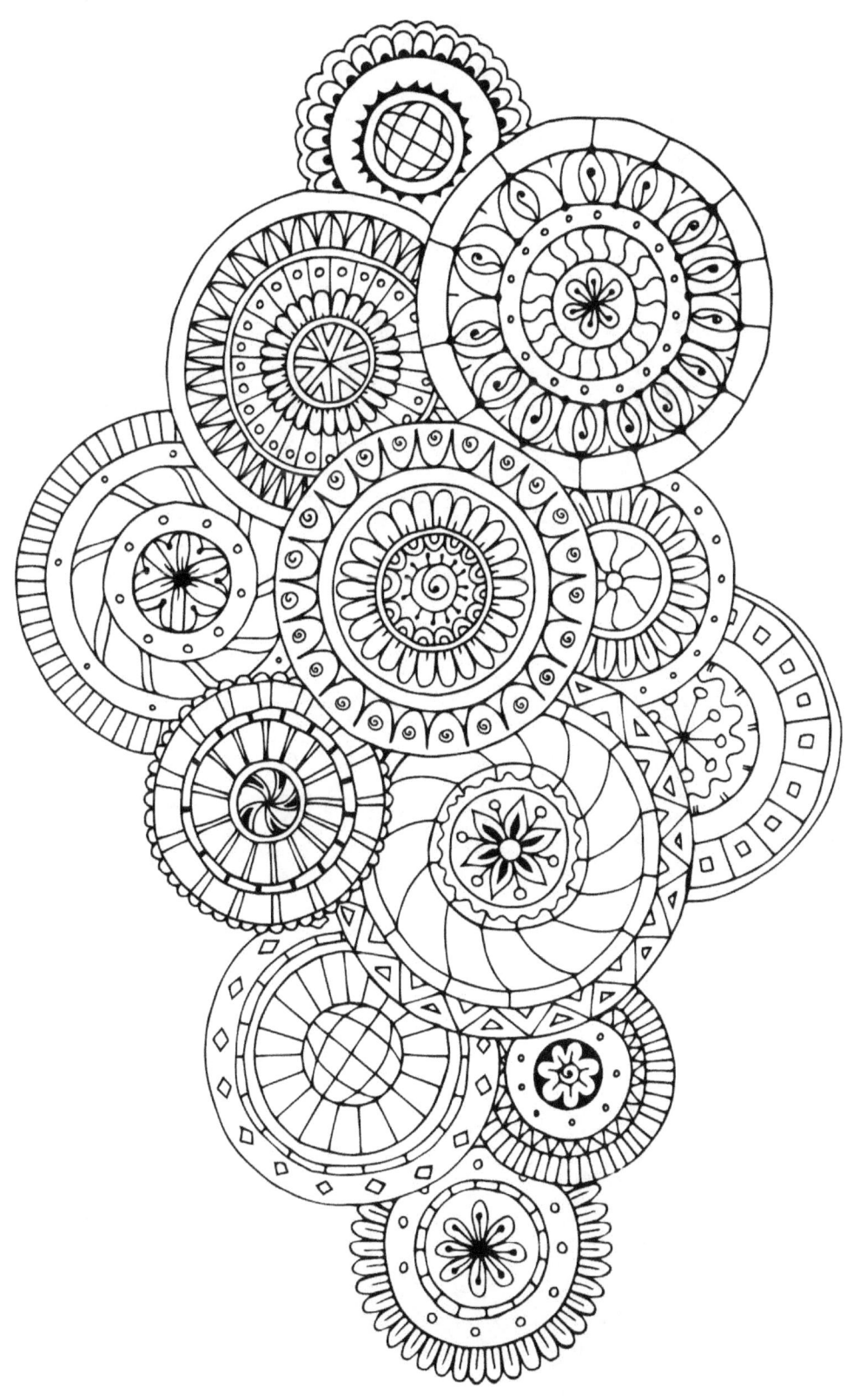

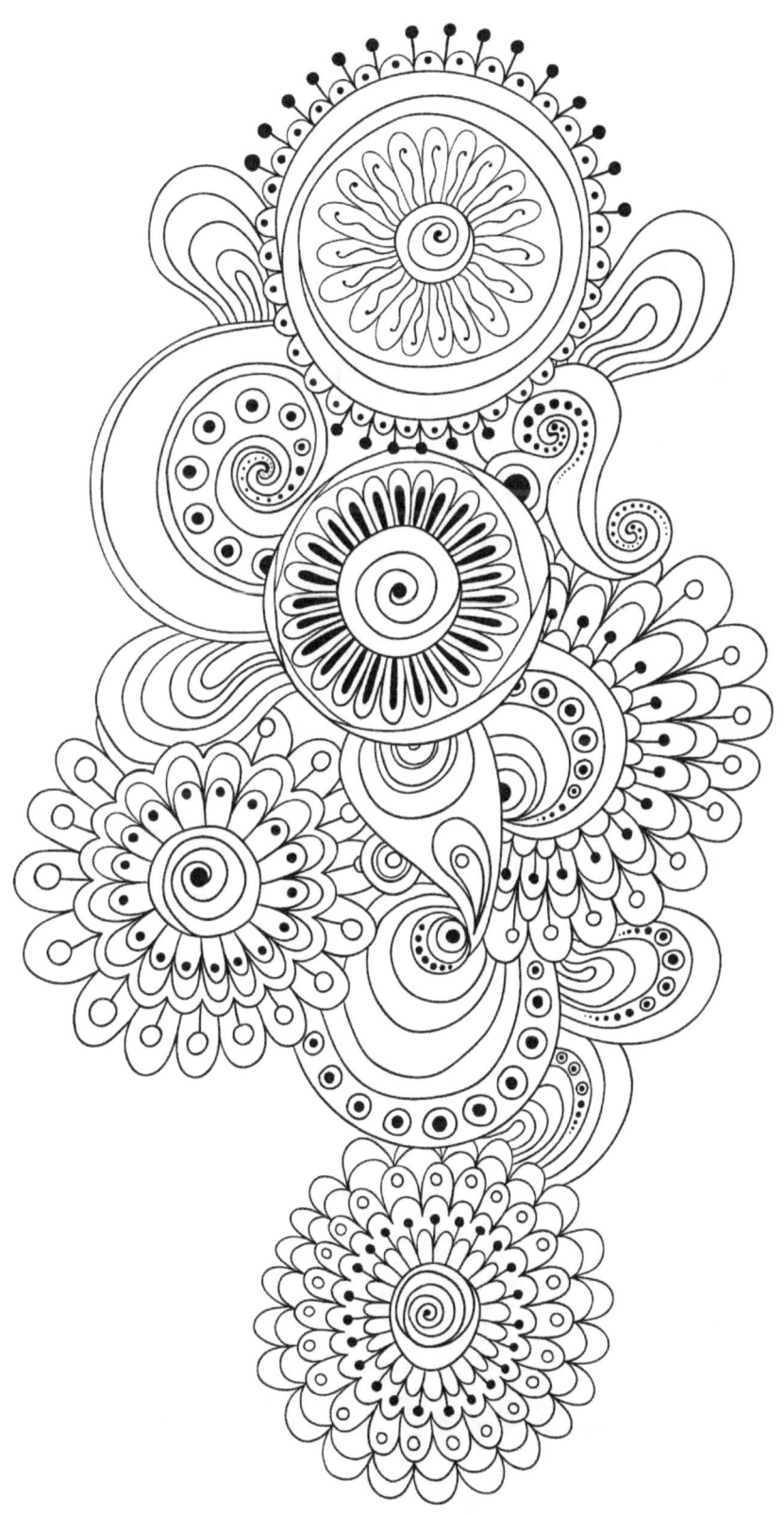

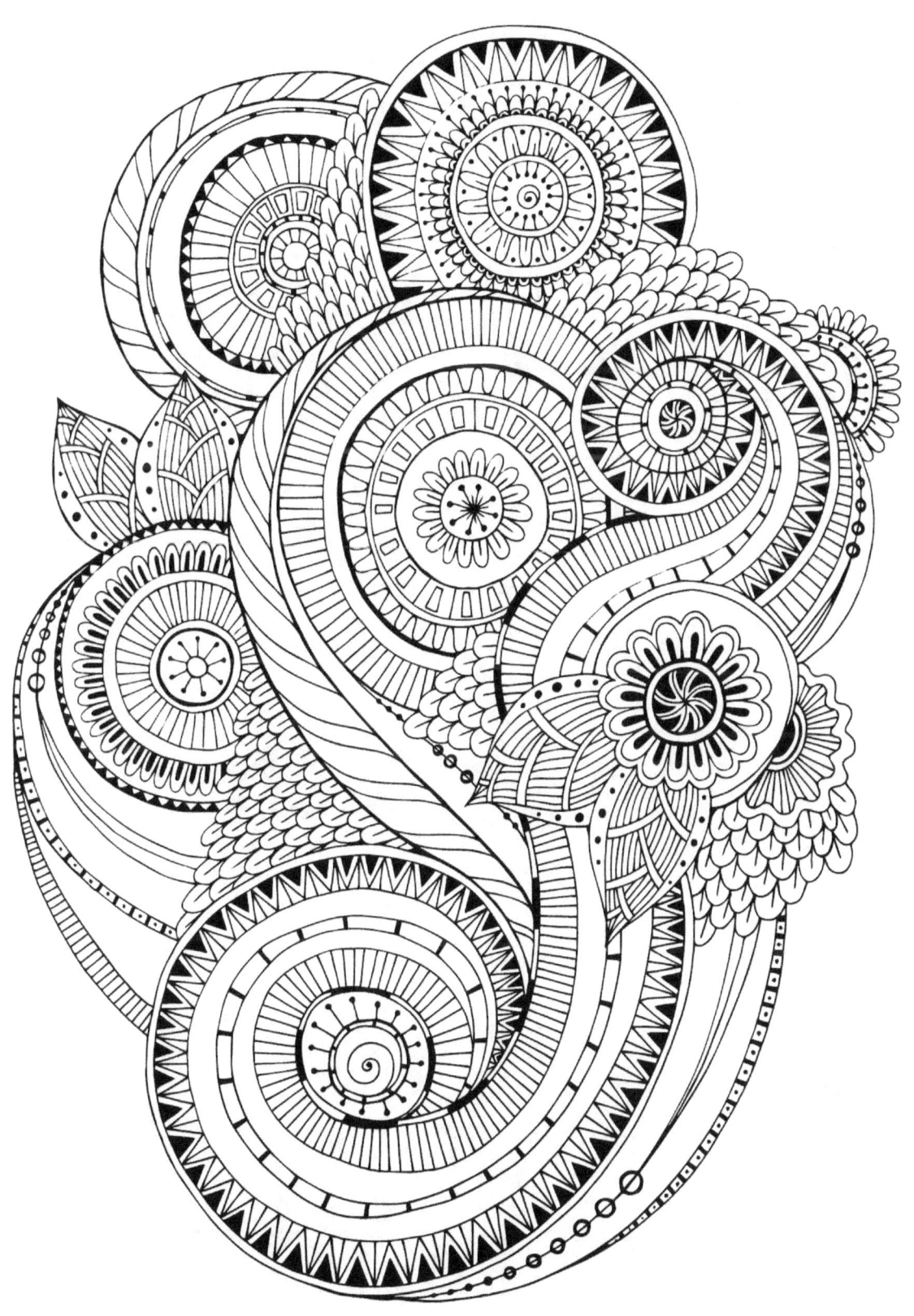

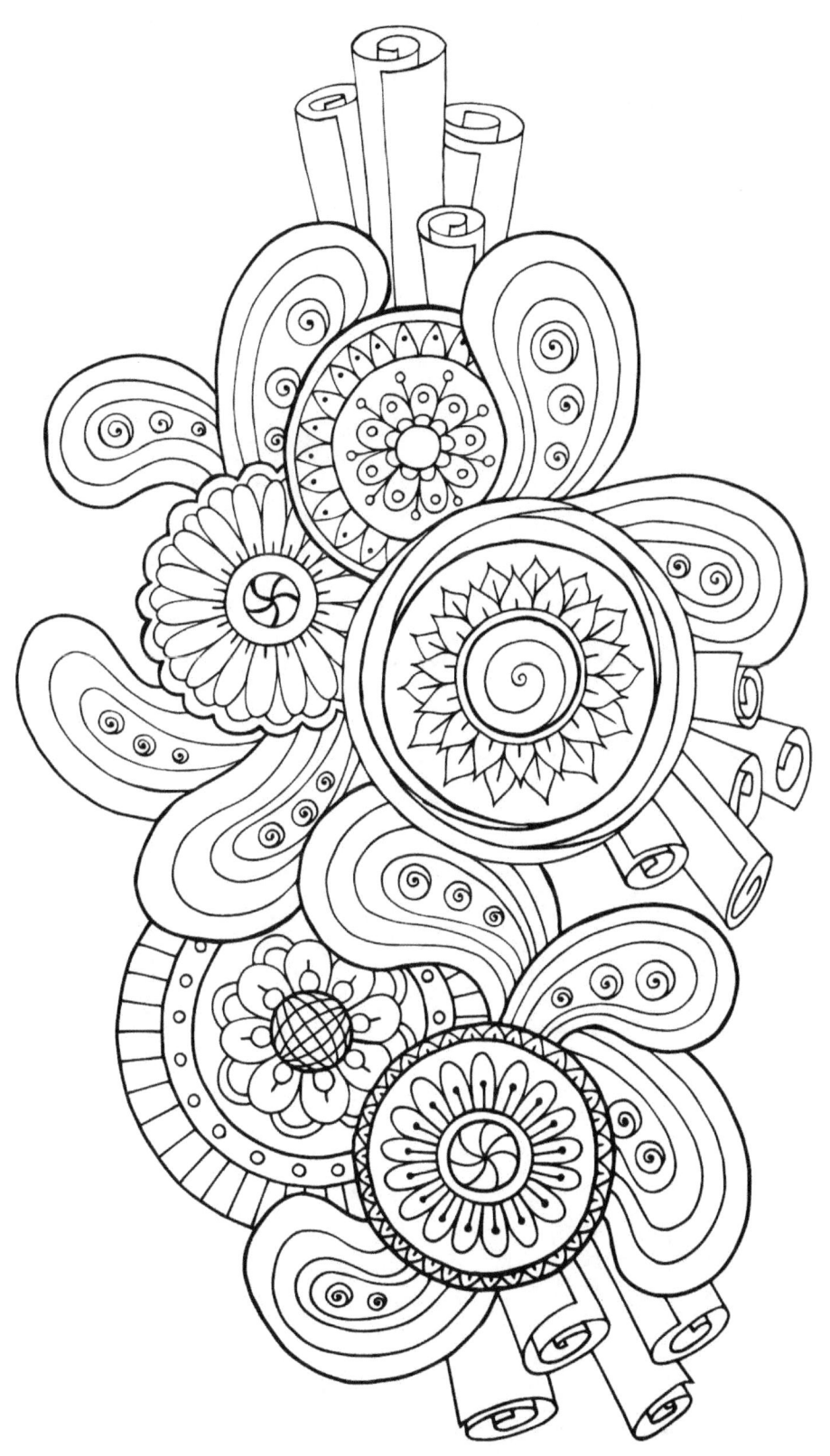

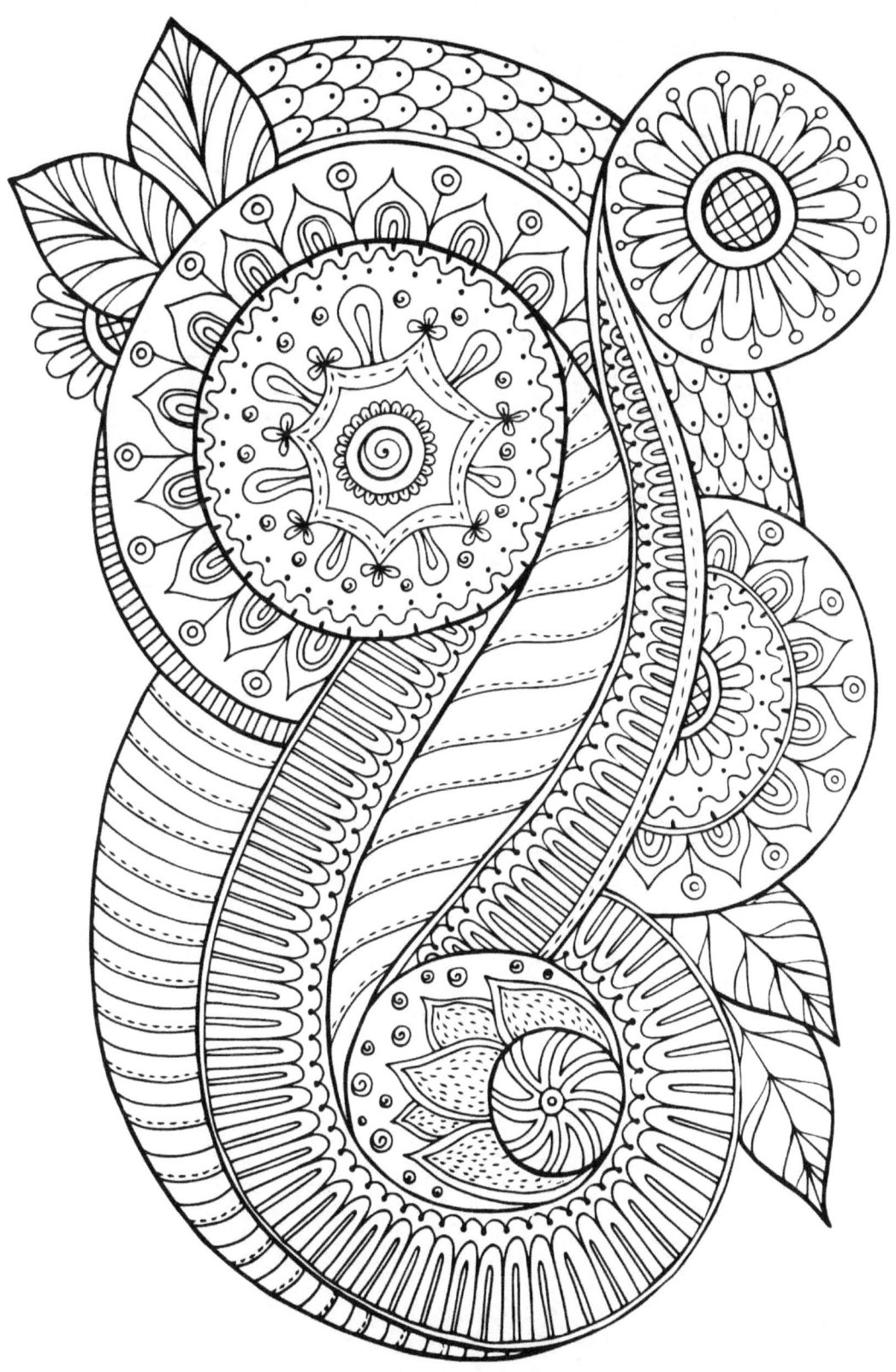

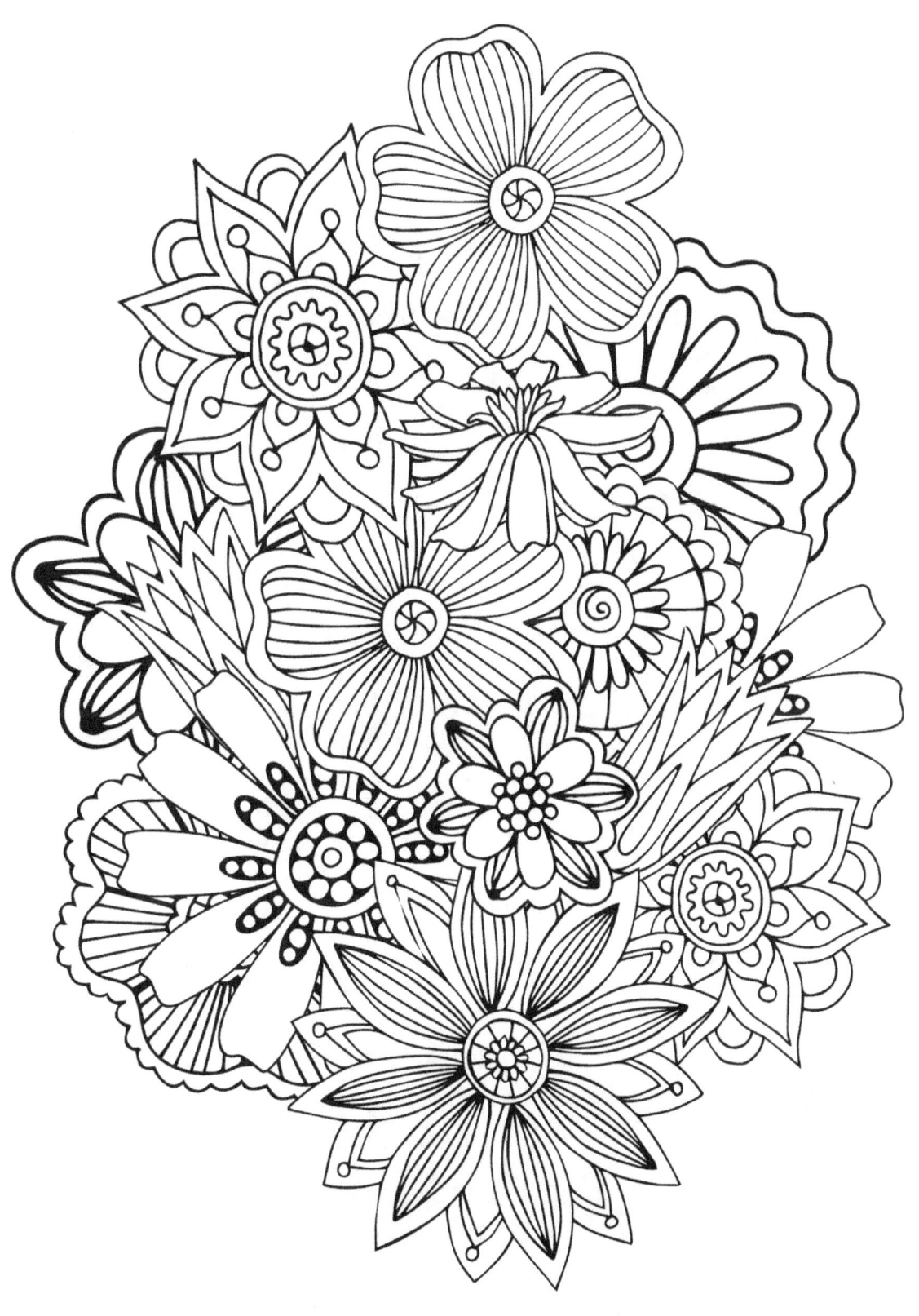

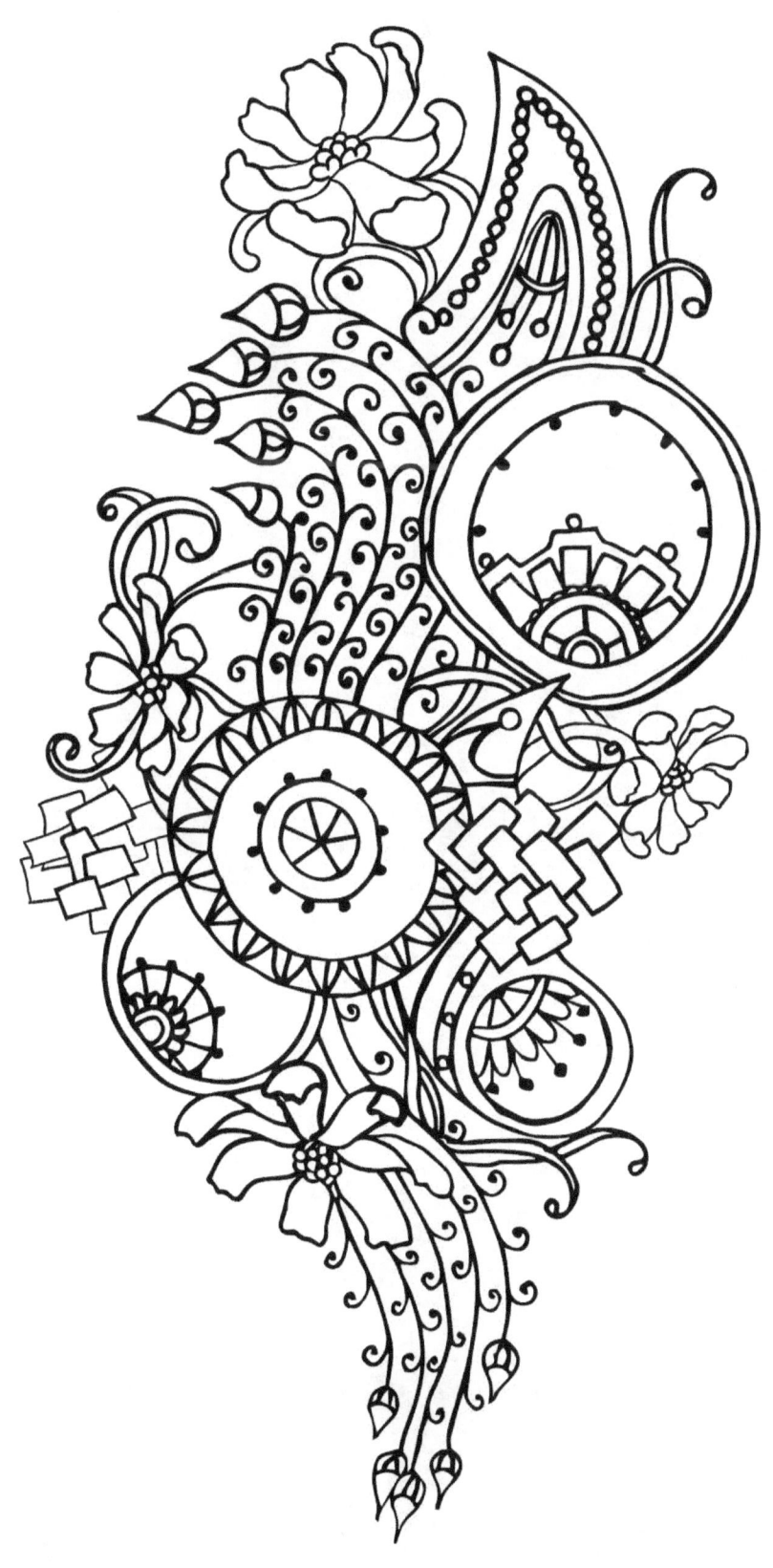

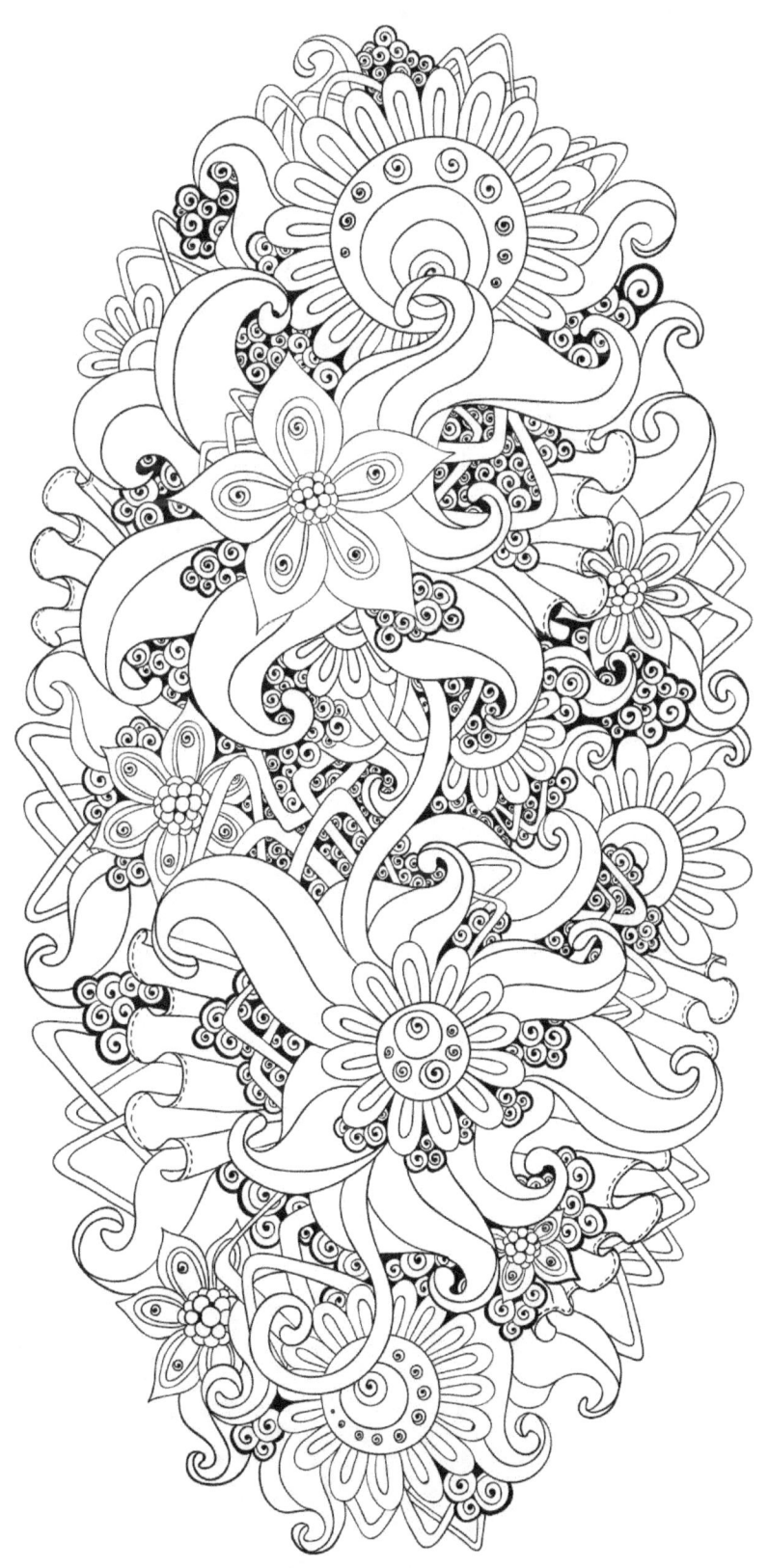

More books from Hobby Habitat

You can find our entire Coloring Books collection on Amazon, just type in

"Hobby Habitat Coloring Books"

in the search box...or *search* for the books bellow by ISBN number!

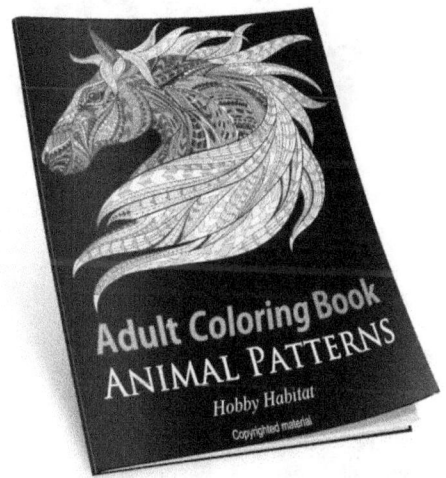

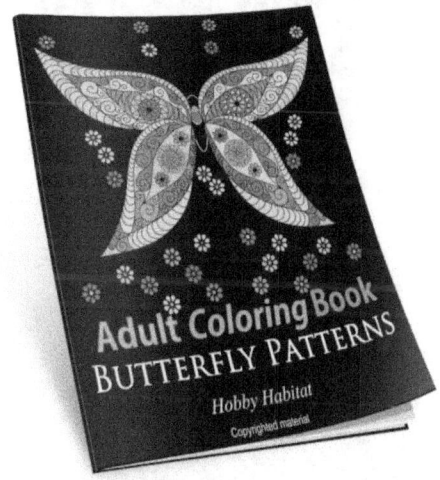

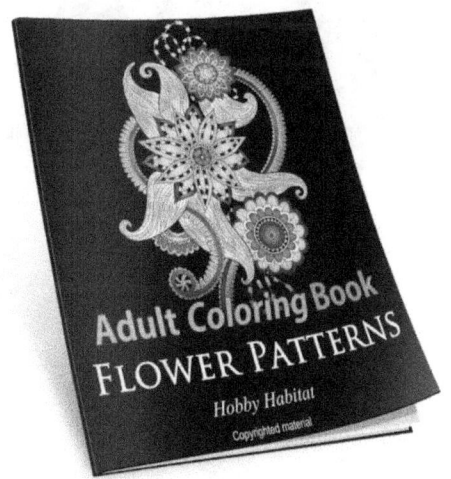

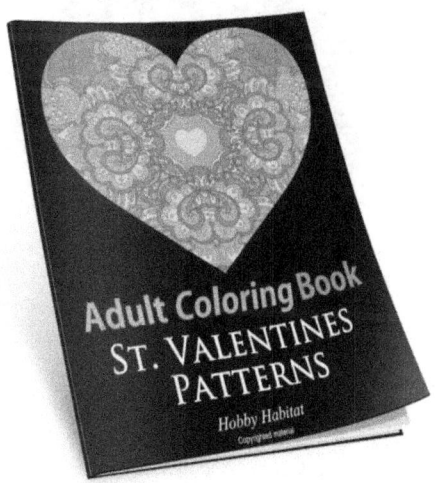

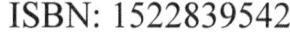

ISBN: 1522839542

ISBN: 1523607149

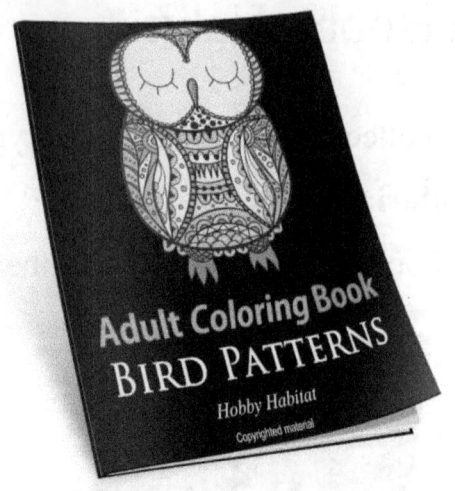

ISBN: 1523617411

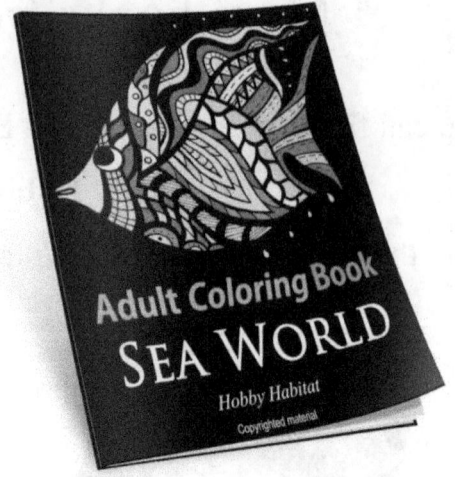

ISBN: 1523608544

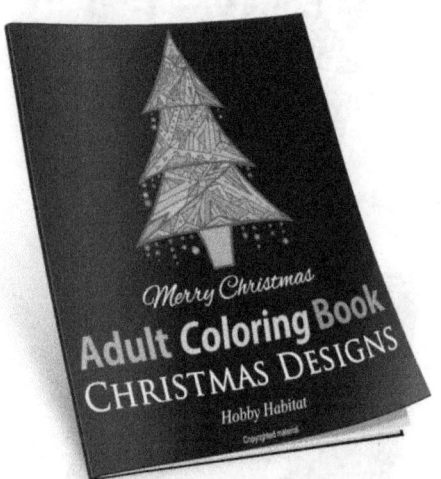

ISBN: 1519755589

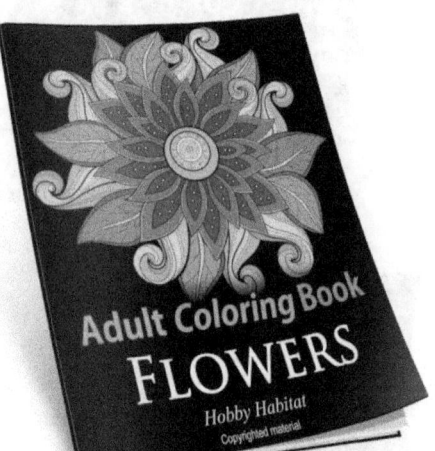

ISBN: 1523898917

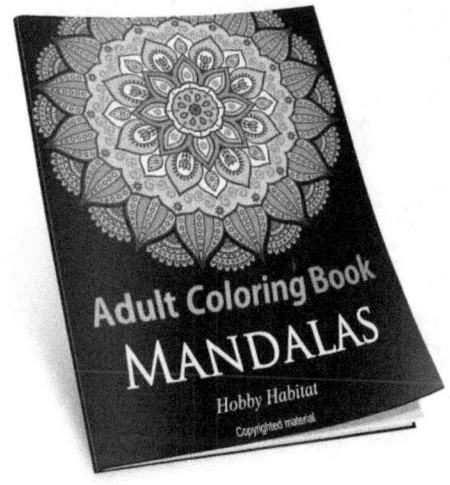

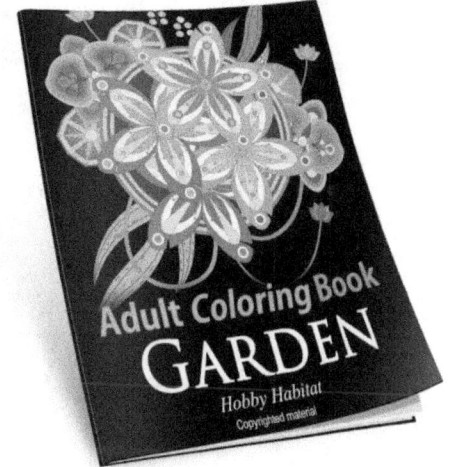

ISBN: 152389900X

ISBN: 1530035554

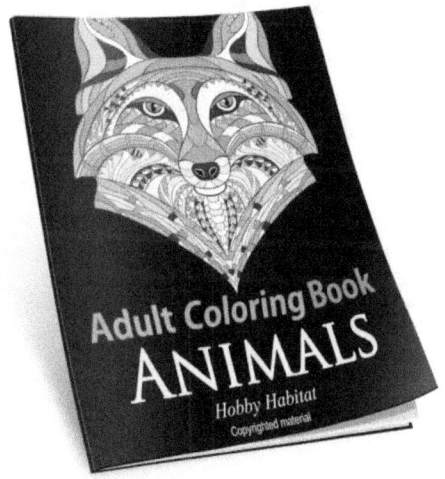

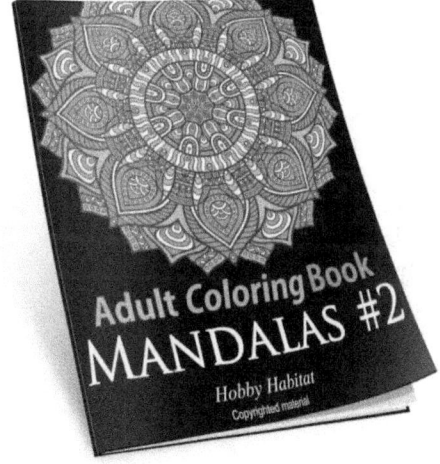

ISBN: 1530035473

ISBN: 1530660955

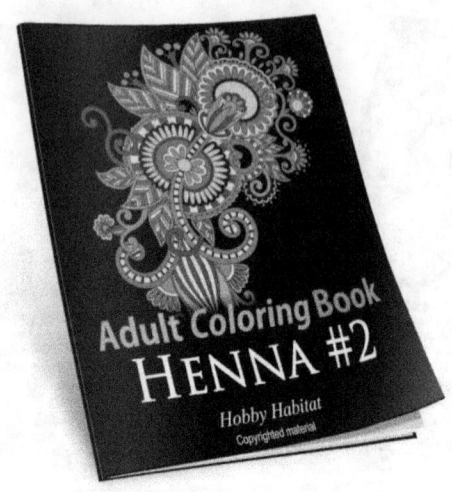

ISBN: 1532707762

From the Author

Thank you for buying and coloring our book, we sincerely hope you have enjoyed it!

Can we ask for a small favor? A lot of work goes in to preparing and publishing our books and honest reviews really do help us, especially when it comes to understanding what we should improve in our books.

If you have a minute, we would really appreciate if you could go to the book store where you have purchased this book and leave a short review…we do actually read our reviews!

Thank you!

Remember also to grab your FREE bonus book at:

www.hobbyhabitat.com/freecoloringbook

www.ingramcontent.com/pod-product-compliance
Lightning Source LLC
Chambersburg PA
CBHW080624190526
45169CB00009B/3284